STAR WARS

MOST WANTED

Written by

RAE CARSON

EGMONT

We bring stories to life

First published in Great Britain 2018
by Egmont UK Limited, The Yellow Building,
1 Nicholas Road, London W11 4AN

Cover design by Richie Hull

© & ™ 2018 Lucasfilm Ltd.

ISBN 978 1 4052 9148 4
67958/001

Printed in UK

To find more great *Star Wars* books, visit
www.egmont.co.uk/starwars

Stay safe online. Any website addresses listed in this book are correct at the time
of going to print. However, Egmont is not responsible for content hosted by third
parties. Please be aware that online content can be subject to change and websites
can contain content that is unsuitable for children. We advise that all children are
supervised when using the internet.

Egmont takes its responsibility to the planet and its inhabitants very seriously.
All the papers we use are from well-managed forests run by responsible suppliers.

For my fellow rebels Hannah Beil and Jacob Beil

CHAPTER 1

Han was late—again. If he missed curfew one more time, there'd be hell to pay.

He ran through the maze of old sewers, thinking of ways he might be able to talk his way past Lady Proxima's guards. A klaxon sounded, echoing through the damp, murky tunnel. The racket startled a clutch of rats, which squealed and skittered over the toe of Han's boot, disappearing into the shadows. The klaxon meant that somewhere above him, on the dark streets of Corellia, a factory had just signaled the end of the night shift. He had mere minutes to get back to the White Worm lair.

Fortunately, Han knew a shortcut. Or—perhaps—unfortunately. The quickest route would take him past Old Man Powlo's hidey-hole. He could handle the old guy, right? Just because a few of Han's fellow White Worms had disappeared in Powlo's territory didn't mean the shortcut wasn't worth the risk. Han's luck would hold. He was sure of it.

A grate appeared on his right, barely more than a dark impression in the stone wall. For the thousandth time,

Han wished Lady Proxima would light these tunnels. But most in her gang were Grindalids, an amphibious species with near perfect nighttime vision. Mere humans didn't warrant such accommodations.

Han crouched before the grate, grabbed it with both hands, and lifted it from its mooring. It moved easily; only a tiny clatter of crumbling mortar gave him away. Han ducked inside and replaced the grate behind him.

Now he had to choose: move quickly or quietly? He couldn't do both.

His stomach growled. His pants were too short on his frame. Maybe he wouldn't be so hungry if he wasn't still growing like a weed. That's why he was supposed to be proving himself to Lady Proxima. The position of Head had recently opened up due to the tragic disappearance of the current Head, and Han needed the promotion desperately—and the extra food ration that came with it.

"Quickly" won.

This tunnel was too low for an all-out sprint, so he hunched his shoulders and pushed forward at a fast jog. It was so dark that he risked missing his turn, so he let his fingertips slide along the wall as he went. The cold stone was slick with something squishy and damp that started to build up under his short nails. He tried not to think about it.

It was a welcome relief when his fingertips met air. He turned right, ducking his head to avoid the low overhang that he couldn't see but knew was there. A sudden scent brought him up short.

The White Worm lair with its many entrances wasn't exactly located in the most fragrant part of Corellia. Word on the street was you could smell a White Worm coming a klick away, thanks to the abandoned buildings and sewers they called home. Han hardly noticed anymore. He was nose-blind to the scents of rot and waste; it was rare for him to smell anything at all down here.

But this was different: sharp and bitter, with a hint of char. Old Man Powlo had found something unspeakable to burn for breakfast. Just as well. It meant that Han was less likely to become breakfast himself.

A few more steps, and a dim glow began to cut through the darkness. The tunnel walls brightened from fathomless black to sticky gray. Here, beneath the oldest part of the city of Coronet, the tunnels were made of duracrete blocks, with dark mold staining the mortar and oozing down the sides. Good thing Han wasn't afraid of a little dirt.

Just a few meters more, and he would be beyond Powlo's lair and home free. The tunnel ceiling became even lower, and Han had no choice but to slow his pace.

The glow sharpened. Light poured from a giant crack

in the wall—large enough for an almost grown man like him to slip through. Instead, he began to tiptoe past.

Against his better judgment, Han found himself peeking inside. He'd seen Old Man Powlo before from a safe distance but never spoken with him. He couldn't help being curious.

The crack opened into a small round cave. A fire pit ringed with cinderblocks took up the center space. Beside it crouched Powlo himself, wild gray hair sticking up at all angles, knobby knees bent practically to his ears as he held something dark to his mouth and crunched noisily. He was skinny and long limbed, clothed in tattered rags. From this distance, lit only by firelight, Powlo seemed human, but Han knew better. No one had any idea what species the old fellow was, or where in the galaxy he'd come from, but he was certainly not human.

Han crept past, toes light, breath measured and soft. The ball of his left foot dislodged a bit of gravel.

It was the slightest sound, hardly noticeable at all, but Powlo whirled, baring sharp teeth. The creature's eyes glowed molten gold around slitted pupils, like those of a venomous snake.

Han froze. His mind told him to flee, but his instincts were commanding him to stay put, that running was the worst thing he could do. Han always trusted his instincts. They'd kept him alive more than once.

They stared at each other for the space of several breaths.

"When in doubt, brazen it out" was Han's motto. So he forced a cheerful smile and said, "Hey, there, pal."

The creature frowned. "Not *pal*," he said. "Powlo." His voice was raspy and thin.

Han blinked. "Right. My mistake. Um, anyway, your breakfast smells"—like rotting fish boiled in bad ale—"really delicious."

Powlo's glowing eyes narrowed. "Won't share. Can't make me."

Han put up his hands. "No problem. I've got breakfast waiting for me back at the lair. Lady Proxima's probably getting worried by now." All lies, of course. Proxima didn't give a rat's whisker about him or anyone, but Powlo didn't need to know that. "Just heard there was a fellow down here. Wanted to stop by and, uh, say hi. Introduce myself. I'm Han."

"Han," Powlo repeated.

"Yep, that's me. And you're Powlo. See? We're friends now."

The fire crackled while Powlo considered this. He took another bite and chewed, his eyes never leaving Han's face.

Han peered carefully at the thing in Powlo's hands. Whatever he was holding had legs. Lots of legs. At least it wasn't a human body part.

"Well, I'd better be on my way," Han said at last. "Or Proxima will come looking for me. Nice meeting you, Powlo." He began to back away from the crack in the wall.

"Wait. Han."

Han froze.

In a plaintive tone, the creature said, "You visit again?"

"Uh, sure. Of course."

Powlo sneered, showing his pointed teeth. No, he was *smiling*. "See soon!" he said.

"You bet," Han replied. He waved jauntily and fled down the corridor toward the White Worm lair. The guard at the gate seemed disappointed when Han slipped through at the last minute, just before he had a chance to lock it.

He'd been right to trust his luck.

Qi'ra reached the head of the mess line. She dipped a ladle into the giant pot and plopped the viscous sludge that passed for breakfast into her bowl. It was grayish-green with dark flecks, and it tasted like mud soaked in brine. But in all her years with the White Worms it had never made her sick, which meant that forcing herself to eat it was the sensible thing to do. Day after day after day.

Of course, if she won the promotion that had just

opened up, she'd get to eat fish for a change. Even an occasional piece of fruit.

Thinking of the promotion made her glance toward the doorway. All the other scrumrats who were under consideration for the job had made it back from the night's errands on time. All except one, that was: a human named Han. She didn't think he'd be much competition, especially if he turned up late yet again. Lady Proxima hated tardiness. More important, she didn't trust anyone who couldn't keep up with her unreasonable demands.

Qi'ra took her bowl to one of the many round tables dotting the mess hall. Each one could sit six humans or Grindalids, and though the tables were made of molding wood, their thick, slightly irregular shapes reminded Qi'ra of giant lily pads. In fact, the entire White Worm den put Qi'ra in mind of a dank swamp—dark walls, wet floors, creeping algae, and even these lily pad tables.

Two others were already seated: Rebolt, a tall, broad-shouldered human boy with a perpetual frown, and Tsuulo, a green-skinned Rodian with one sagging antenna, whose cheerful disposition almost made up for the fact that Qi'ra could hardly understand a word he said.

"Han's not back yet," Rebolt observed while Qi'ra settled herself at the table.

"Indeed," Qi'ra said. "Late again."

"Good," Rebolt said, then shoved a spoonful of sludge into his mouth.

Along with her and Han, Rebolt and Tsuulo were the most likely candidates for the promotion. Rebolt probably figured Han was his toughest competition. Qi'ra took a bite of sludge to hide her smile. He had no idea who his real competition was.

Tsuulo twittered a question in Huttese.

"They're *hounds*, not dogs," Rebolt replied, bristling. "And they're in the kennel, getting fed."

"Those biscuits you feed them are better than this," Qi'ra mumbled, letting a glop of porridge fall from her spoon and back into the bowl.

Rebolt's hounds almost never left his side. They were fierce, enormous beasts who drooled almost as much as they ate, and Qi'ra was not sad that Rebolt had come to breakfast without them this time.

Tsuulo said something else. All Qi'ra understood was "Han," but Rebolt's head shot up. Qi'ra followed his gaze toward the entrance, and sure enough, Han himself was barreling through. He was dirty and disheveled, with sewer mud caking his boots.

The curfew alarm pealed.

"Figures," Rebolt grumbled. "Just in time."

Qi'ra shared his disgust, but she kept her face emotionless. She always kept her face emotionless.

"Someone needs to find out where he goes," Rebolt said. "Why he's late or almost late all the time."

Rebolt wanted dirt on him. Something that would disqualify Han for the job of Head. Qi'ra didn't like Han any more than Rebolt did, but he'd get no help from her.

She kept an eye on Han as he hurried through the line, got his bowlful of sludge and brought it to their table. "Hey," Han said.

"Hey," they responded in unison.

The four of them almost always sat together. It wasn't like they were friends or anything, but they were among the oldest in the gang and among the first accepted into the White Worms who weren't actually Grindalids. They had survived a long time in this place. So they tended to stick together.

They ate mostly in silence. The other White Worms watched them from their own tables. Things had been tense lately. Everyone in the lair knew one of the four was most likely to get the position of Head. The Grindalids hated the idea of taking orders from a human or Rodian. It made sense, though. Grindalids needed environment suits to be on Corellia's surface for any length of time. Their white, segmented carapaces couldn't handle too much dry air or light. But a human or Rodian could conduct business anywhere, anytime, without an expensive suit to maintain, which was why Lady Proxima had been recruiting so many humans the past few years. Naming one of them Head was the right strategic move for her.

"So, Han," Rebolt began, and Qi'ra winced with the sure knowledge that Rebolt was about to be clumsy and arrogant and pretty much eaten alive by the much cleverer Han.

"Rebolt," Han said around a mouthful of sludge.

"You were almost late. Again."

"You call it *almost late*, but I call it *on time*. I was on time. Again."

"Where do you go all the time? What's so important that you'd risk curfew?"

"Wow, is it just me, or is the sludge particularly fishy today?" Han said.

"Very fishy," Qi'ra agreed. Han had a way of throwing people off guard. Rebolt was trying to be assertive, but in just a few sentences, Han would turn the tables. She used to believe it was all part of a careful strategy of Han's, but now she knew better. There was nothing strategic about Han; everything he did was born of instinctive reflex.

Tsuulo said something, but Qi'ra only understood the word for "burn."

"Yep," Han agreed. "Definitely overcooked."

Rebolt's frown deepened. "Don't change the subject. I want to know where you were."

Han scraped around his bowl with his spoon. "No dogs today? Did something happen to them?"

Rebolt bristled; Tsuulo twittered something.

"Oh, right. My mistake," Han said. "*Hounds*, not dogs."

Qi'ra understood Rebolt's desire to find out where Han went; if he was running extra errands for Lady Proxima or doing something that gave him an advantage, then Qi'ra wanted to know too. But Rebolt's direct line of attack was always doomed to fail, and he couldn't see it.

"I'm going to tell Lady Proxima she should have you followed," Rebolt said.

"You do that," Han said. "You waste Proxima's resources like that and you're bound to stay a scrumrat forever."

Rebolt began to protest but Qi'ra set her bowl down loudly. The other three looked at her.

"Everyone has secrets," she said to Rebolt. If a direct line of attack didn't work, sometimes you had to come at things sideways instead. "As you pointed out, no one knows where Han goes after his shift."

Han narrowed his eyes at her, not sure where she was going with this. *Good*, she thought.

"For another example," she continued calmly, "no

one knows why Tsuulo's left antenna is drooping. He's too young. Something happened to him."

Tsuulo frowned.

"For yet another example, no one knows where your hounds came from, Rebolt, or how a poor White Worm kid like you can afford to feed and train them."

The side of Han's mouth turned up into a tiny half smile.

"So, I suggest you let it go," Qi'ra said, "or someone might be tempted to ask *you* some uncomfortable questions."

"Are you threatening me?" Rebolt asked.

Qi'ra tried to appear affronted. "Of course not. I'm *helping* you. And you're welcome."

Rebolt looked back and forth between her and Han, but he chose to be uncharacteristically wise and said nothing.

Han leaned toward her and said, "Does that mean you have a secret too, Qi'ra?"

His face still wore a lopsided grin. She hated that grin. It made her want to punch him in the face.

"*Everyone* has secrets," she said evenly. The trick with Han was not to let him put you on the defensive. "If I told you mine, I'd just have to go find new ones."

His eyes did not leave her face as she turned her attention back to her bowl of sludge.

Tsuulo said something that made both boys snicker.

"What did he say?" Qi'ra demanded. "Tsuulo, what did you say?"

"He said it's no secret that you look lovely today," Rebolt offered. "Isn't that right, Han?"

Han nodded. "And that you are the jewel of the White Worm lair. Also not a secret."

"And that the Corellian sun is a dark shadow compared to your . . ." Rebolt began gamely. "Uh, something really bright."

Tsuulo was laughing now.

"Fine, don't tell me," Qi'ra said, making sure her face displayed a slight frown. But letting them joke at her expense was a good thing. It would put them at ease. Lure them into underestimating her.

A commotion across the room got their attention. The round hatch to the inner sanctum swung open. A pair of small Grindalids entered the room and stared threateningly over the pale white beaks of their faces. They were followed by Moloch, Lady Proxima's right-hand Worm. He was still wearing an envirosuit, a set of brown robes bleached grayish white from sewer pollutants. The robes were insulated with layers of moist air. A vaporizer rested around his neck, blowing mist up at his wrinkled white skin and long nostril slits. In one hand he carried an ivory-colored shockstaff—a staff that occasionally appeared in Qi'ra's nightmares. From a distance it seemed beautiful, sculpted in flowing lines like flowers or vines. But up close, the vines became limbs and tentacles that swirled around the staff's tip as though writhing in pain and horror.

Moloch must have just returned from the surface. Qi'ra wondered where he'd been and what secrets *he* was keeping.

"Han," he bellowed.

Han flinched, and his bowl clattered on the table, drawing Moloch's attention. The Grindalid strode toward them, robes dragging on the ground.

"Ha!" smirked Rebolt. "You're in trouble for being late after all."

Qi'ra almost felt sorry for Han. Proxima never fetched someone after shift unless something was wrong. Well, at least he'd be no competition for *her* job.

"And Qi'ra," Moloch said as he reached their table. "Lady Proxima wishes to speak to you both."

Qi'ra's heart dropped into her belly as she and Han shared a terrified glance.

Reluctantly, she rose from the table. A few bites of sludge remained in her bowl. Tsuulo reached for it, giving her a tentative look. She nodded permission; her appetite had fled anyway.

Han pushed his bowl over too. "Here you go, pal." The Rodian's snout turned up into what was, for him, a huge grin.

Han stood. "Let's get this over with."

Rebolt scooted his chair back and rose as if to accompany them, but Moloch shoved him back down. "Just Han and Qi'ra," he growled.

Rebolt tensed, as though ready to fight back, but Moloch was bigger than Rebolt to the same degree that Rebolt was bigger than all the other human kids, and Rebolt never picked a fight he might lose. "What? Why just them?"

"None of your business, scrumrat."

"Whatever they can do for her, I can do better! I'm loyal, punctual, and—"

Moloch cuffed the back of his head. "Your hounds are hungry."

"W-what?"

"Go feed your hounds," Moloch ordered. "Or I'll feed you to them."

Rebolt froze, then nodded assent. Qi'ra would trade places with him in a nanosecond if she could. He clearly thought this strange daytime meeting conferred some kind of privilege. Qi'ra knew it meant trouble. Based on the grave look on Han's face, he knew it too.

"With me. Now," Moloch said to Han and Qi'ra. Then he turned and walked away without a backward glance, fully expecting to be obeyed.

Tsuulo ignored them all, happily shoving the extra sludge into his mouth, but she felt Rebolt seething at their backs as she and Han followed Moloch to the audience chamber.

Two White Worm guards stood outside the massive door hatch. A bulkhead door, no less, tarnish staining the edges. These tunnels and underground chambers were old; rumor was the gang's lair used to be a massive manufacturing site. A few rooms still housed defunct machinery—hulking steel stamp presses, a few lathes, and even an industrial-sized holding tank that was empty of everything but rust.

Some of the dim overhead lighting still worked because Tsuulo—the den's resident genius—had illegally tapped into the power grid of a nearby factory. In addition, three sump pumps kept groundwater at bay. But only three. The lair actually contained five sump pumps, but the White Worms purposely kept two turned off. As a result, the audience hall, known to the kids as the Sinkhole, was meters deep in slimy, rusty water.

Beyond the door hatch was a round tunnel leading to Lady Proxima's underground pond.

Qi'ra and Han stepped forward to enter, but Moloch

put a huge hand on Han's shoulder, stopping him in his tracks.

"Qi'ra enters alone," he said to Han. "You'll go in after."

She and Han shared another startled look. Moloch prodded her forward, and she stepped into the wet air of the tunnel. Alone.

She strode forward confidently—one thing she knew was, the more nervous you felt, the more confident you needed to seem—until the tunnel ended at the edge of the pond. The walls of the Sinkhole rose around her, giving the impression of a long-lost ventilation shaft stretching for the surface and fresh air. Morning light filtered through a few narrow windows at the top of the shaft, like a promise of something better, but the windows were mostly painted over in black so that only a few motes of brightness reached the bottom.

Qi'ra focused all her attention on the only thing that mattered. Lady Proxima had emerged from the middle of the cistern, like a Grindalid castle surrounded by a greasy moat. She wore an outfit that was half body armor, half jewelry, all of it made from pieces of machinery scavenged from the factories of Corellia. As if, even though she was forced to live underground, she was determined to turn the industry of this planet into her own source of strength and fortune.

Qi'ra admired that. She saw a role model before her.

Lady Proxima stared down at Qi'ra, flexing the claws of her dominant arms. The bone-white beak of her face looked like an ax, ready to fall on the nearest target. When she smiled, the wet line of her mouth gleamed like the edge of a sawtoothed blade. No doubt Lady Proxima intended the gesture to be reassuring.

"So nice to see you, Qi'ra, my darling," she hissed.

"Good morning, Lady," Qi'ra replied with perfect poise, though her heart was a drum in her chest.

Lady Proxima glanced around the room at her loyal soldiers. Qi'ra couldn't tell if she was going to dismiss them or order them to attack.

The hatch door slammed shut behind her.

Han did not care for this situation one bit. He stared at the hatch, hoping Qi'ra was all right.

Not that he cared much for the girl; she was stuck-up, hard to read, and way too smart. She tried to keep a low profile, but Han knew Qi'ra was his toughest competition for the position of Head. It would make his life a lot easier if something unlucky happened to her.

But he couldn't bring himself to wish misfortune on her. Qi'ra might be snobbish and inscrutable, but she had never been unkind to him. Unlike Rebolt and

Moloch. Besides, she wasn't hard to look at. Also unlike Rebolt and Moloch.

The moments ticked by interminably. At his back were the sounds of bowls being cleared away, chairs scooting, White Worms chattering. The noises gradually faded as everyone finished breakfast and made their way to the bunk room or tunnels to catch some sleep before the Corellian day turned to night and everyone would be sent out to work again.

Soon Han was all alone in the mess hall, with the exception of Moloch and the two silent White Worms guarding the door to the Sinkhole.

A ratcatcher droid scooted past his boots. The tiny little tank had been a janitor droid at one point, but Tsuulo had repurposed it to catch vermin. The lair had a tiny fleet of ratcatcher droids now, and they could be counted on to snag several screerats and vervikks per day, which the White Worms used to add some much-needed protein to their breakfast sludge.

Han sighed. He really needed that Head position, if only so he could eat something besides rat porridge.

"So," Han said to the guards, just to fill the silence. His voice seemed too loud to his own ears in the empty, echoing mess hall. "Long night?"

Moloch made a clicking sound that could have been a threat or possibly just something stuck in his teeth, but otherwise didn't respond. The other Worms said nothing, just stared straight ahead as if he wasn't there.

"Any idea what Lady Proxima wants with Qi'ra and me?" he tried again.

One of the Worms looked down at him with disdain, but said nothing.

Han tried one last time, because talking was way better than this horrible waiting. "So, hey, a few of us have a sabacc game going in the bunk room. We play every night before shift. You should join us sometime."

Still nothing.

"I'm just starting to learn. Do you know how to play sabacc?"

He might as well have been talking to a wall. Or three walls even. Han shrugged. You couldn't blame a guy for trying.

The door flew open, and a rush of wet, warm air almost made him sneeze. Qi'ra barreled out, her eyes as unknowable as always, but her shoulders were tense, her mouth stubbornly set. She was a petite brunette, almost a whole head shorter than Han, but somehow her presence could fill a whole room. Something about that made him uneasy.

"Qi'ra? You okay?"

She ignored him, rushing past without looking right or left, and headed for the tunnel leading into the sewers.

"Nice talking to you too!" he called after her.

"Get inside, scrumrat," Moloch said, shoving Han with the butt of his horrible shockstaff.

Han put his hands up. "All right, all right, I'm going." He stepped into the tunnel, and the door slammed shut behind him.

Lady Proxima rose from the middle of the Sinkhole, water lapping at the pond's edges. She wore nothing but chains and metal plates, which seemed impractical to Han. She must get very cold, and all that ironwork seemed like it would rust in the damp air and chafe her skin. Definitely not for him. He'd much rather have boots that kept his feet dry and a thick jacket for warmth. But to each their own. He wasn't about to judge.

The water rippled with movement, and Han was reminded that hidden in the murky pond beneath the giant Grindalid was Proxima's latest brood. He had no idea how many she hatched at a time—maybe hundreds of tiny worms, all clamoring for food and space. He was glad they were mostly restful now, that he couldn't see them.

The rest of the room was empty. Not even Proxima's top lieutenants were in attendance. It made the back of Han's neck itch, because the Sinkhole was always filled with Worms. Some even slept here. For some reason, Proxima had sent them away.

"Han, my dear boy," she began. "I have a special assignment for you."

"Of course, Lady," he said quickly. "Whatever you need." But his heart was sinking. Whatever the assignment was, she didn't want anyone to know about it. Which meant it was dangerous and she considered him expendable. He was nothing more than a human scrumrat to her. So much for that promotion.

Not to mention the lost sleep. Proxima kept him busy every night, running him around Coronet to collect payments, gather information, or fetch small shipments. After that, of course, he had a bit of his own business to attend to, which almost always resulted in an all-out sprint to get back to the lair before curfew. Sometimes he could barely stay awake through breakfast. It was a relief to fall into his damp, filthy bunk every morning.

But there would be no sleep for him today.

"I want you to go to the Foundry," she said.

"Sure. No problem." He'd been to the Foundry plenty of times. He even had a friend there.

"Take the tunnels and enter through the basement. The access hatch will be unlocked for you."

"Access hatch. Got it."

She leaned forward on her pedestal and made a sharp clicking sound. It was the noise Grindalids made when they were hungry. "Han, my boy, you must not be seen entering or leaving. No matter what. Do you understand?"

He blinked. "Sure. I can do that." The Foundry employed thousands of Corellians, churning out basic starship components for the Empire and other interests on its massive assembly lines. Even the basement might be occupied. He swallowed hard. "No problem. Do you want me to fetch something? Or is there a message you want me—"

She hissed, cutting him off, then said, "No questions, boy. Not this time."

Han pressed his lips together and waited.

"In the basement," she continued, "you'll meet a contact. He will ask what you've been up to. You're to say that you've been dusting crops, the easiest job in the galaxy. Now say it back to me."

"I've been dusting crops, the easiest job in the galaxy."

"Good boy. If you don't say those exact words . . . Well, I will miss you tremendously."

"I . . . see." It was as he feared. She was sending him on this errand because she considered him expendable.

"After you've given the code phrase," Lady Proxima said, "you'll receive further instructions, which you will follow exactly. Do you understand?"

"Yes, Honored Lady." A thin film of sweat was collecting at his hairline.

"I'm sending you because I need someone I trust to be discreet. You must tell no one about this errand, and you must stay alert at all times. There could be . . . complications."

He opened his mouth to ask what kind of complications, but slammed it closed when he remembered that he wasn't supposed to be asking questions.

"You know how much I care for all my children," Lady Proxima said. "And it pains me to send my darling human boy on such a dangerous mission. But if all goes well and you do exactly as you're told and return to me . . ." She paused a moment, letting him wonder. "I am prepared to name you Head of the White Worms."

He almost gasped aloud, not believing his luck. Suddenly, the most dangerous assignment he'd ever received had become the greatest opportunity of his life. He could do this. He had to. Sleep could wait.

"Don't disappoint me, darling," she said, using her best approximation of a mother's loving gaze. Han knew better than to trust that gaze. Whenever she looked at him that way, he felt like a juicy spider about to get pounced on by a monkey lizard.

He said, "Have I ever let you down, Honored Lady?"

She smiled again and the corners of her eyes wrinkled. Lady Proxima pretended to be above the opinions of everyone, especially her White Worm children, but she liked to be flattered. Then she waved a pale, segmented hand at him and said, "Now get out of my sight. I need my rest."

"Yes, Lady."

The hatch opened for him, and he backed out of the Sinkhole, bowing as he went.

When it shut, he leaned against it and took a deep breath. He hated bowing. He hated telling Lady Proxima everything she wanted to hear. He hated being such a toady. Sure, it was a calculated decision, essential to his survival as a Corellian scrumrat. But it felt wrong. Totally against his nature.

If he got that position of Head, he'd finally have some authority. Some freedom. Not to mention better food and sleep. Maybe a new pair of boots. And he could finally tell that jerk Rebolt to—

"Move it, Han," Moloch said. He lifted his shockstaff to point the way. A simple gesture, not intended as a threat. "You have work to do."

Han took off at a jog toward the exact same tunnel Qi'ra had entered just minutes before. What had Proxima said to her? Qi'ra almost never showed discomposure. So by the look on her face, it must have been something awful. He hoped the girl was okay.

He ducked into the sewer and headed for the Foundry.

CHAPTER 2

Qi'ra located the stash right where Lady Proxima had said it would be, at the sewer exit near the Green. It was a nondescript pack made of waterproof leather. Inside was the outfit Proxima had promised—a sturdy knee-length skirt over black leggings, a beautiful bright red top that made Qi'ra gasp with pleasure, and a beige flight jacket that would hit her waist perfectly. She lifted the clothes to her nose and sniffed. They had been sprayed with some kind of floral perfume to cover up the rotten smell of the sewers. It was going to be the nicest thing she'd ever worn. Maybe, when this was all over, she'd get to keep it.

Qi'ra changed quickly, paused a moment to admire the color of the top—such a gorgeous, saturated red!—then swung the gate open and stepped into the sunshine.

Well, "sunshine" was overstating it. It was a typical, gloomy Corellian day, full of clouds and haze. Decades of industry had given the sky a reddish-brown cast, and Qi'ra sometimes felt as though the whole world was going to rust.

But compared with the sewers at night, it felt brighter than a sun.

The sewer itself drained into a small artificial creek running through a grassy park. It was one of the few areas of green space left in Coronet City, located on the outskirts of the capital, far from the scents of fish and exhaust steam and sewage. The green space existed only because the posh hotels surrounding it—which catered to Imperial dignitaries and other influential business entities—felt it was important for their guests to have something beautiful to look at.

More important, the surrounding thick foliage made it the perfect egress for White Worms who needed to reach the edge of town without being seen.

Today, though, Qi'ra was supposed to be seen.

It was the strangest thing, she mused, as she peeked around the bushes and waited for a good opportunity to blend into the crowd of pedestrians. Lady Proxima had never before asked her to be *noticeable*. "I need someone attractive for this assignment," she'd said. "Someone poised. You need to be *seen* entering and leaving the hotel."

Qi'ra found the idea strangely thrilling, not having to hide. And the message she was supposed to give . . . It was the oddest, most exhilarating thing. She couldn't wait for the words to come out of her mouth.

The most amazing thing of all, though, was Lady Proxima's promise. If all went well, Qi'ra would be promoted to the position of Head. She could hardly believe her luck. It was an incredible opportunity, and her entire focus for the next few hours would be on making it happen.

The foot traffic had thinned. Qi'ra threw back her shoulders, raised her head high, and stepped from the trees onto the cobbled path as though she had every right to be there.

One person—a human woman with blond hair—gave her an odd look, but no one else seemed to notice that she'd come from the direction of the creek. She strode forward with purpose, pretending to be oblivious to everyone else. She couldn't help observing, though, that while her bright red shirt was the nicest thing she'd ever owned—not that she owned it *yet*—she was still underdressed. Only Corellia's richest residents lived in this district.

Qi'ra followed the path toward her destination—the Buckell Center, a massive hotel and business complex. It was one of the largest buildings on the planet, a sprawling edifice with multiple wings that hugged one of the city's few hills like a giant, shining spider. Supposedly, it was the only building on Corellia that rivaled the luxury and beauty of those on Coruscant.

Or so Tsuulo had told them all. He'd been born on

Coruscant, so he would know. Or maybe that had been a tall tale to impress everyone.

The tree-lined path ended abruptly, and Qi'ra found herself confronting the main thoroughfare. Landspeeders whizzed by, many of them sleek and beautiful and not at all like the ones she was used to seeing around town. A holoboard ahead flashed an advertisement for a home air filter, guaranteed to protect children from Corellian pollution. In the distance, the sky buzzed with ships taking off and landing at the spaceport.

A well-lit pedestrian tunnel allowed her to cross the thoroughfare. She strode through it as though she belonged and emerged at a wide colonnade leading to the Buckell Center. The sight gave her a start.

Framing the entry were two massive turrets, each the size of a small freighter. They hummed and hissed, pivoting on their bases. Qi'ra kept her head high, her stride purposeful, as she walked between them.

One turned toward her, and her breath hitched. Lights flashed, and the gun barrel crackled with electricity. After a moment, it turned away, choosing to evaluate another pedestrian.

Qi'ra kept going as if nothing had happened, but her mind was reeling. Defensive smart turrets at the Buckell Center! What did it mean? Nothing good, that was for sure.

She dodged a few luxury speeders that were dropping off guests, and she was almost to the entrance when darkness descended all around, like a blanket had been thrown over the sun.

Several people gasped. Even the protocol droid at the valet booth looked up. Qi'ra followed his gaze.

An Imperial Star Destroyer had pulled in overhead and hovered in the sky. Tsuulo had told them that to hover safely, a Star Destroyer had to remain in the planet's mesosphere. Yet even at that distance, it was large enough to turn day into night.

It was not the first Destroyer she'd seen. They were becoming an all-too-common sight in the Corellian skies as more and more of the planet's factories began to manufacture components specifically for Imperial projects. But it still made her shudder, because it seemed like an omen. Between that and the turrets, Qi'ra was on high alert when she finally strode through the glass doors and entered the complex.

Her stride faltered. Never had she seen such luxury. Golden highlights sparkled on every surface and framed every painting and mirror. The potted fruit trees could double their breakfast rations back in the lair. The couches scattered in groups around the lobby looked more comfortable than any bed she had ever slept in.

Maybe she could acquire a couple of throw pillows on her way out. . . .

But that wasn't why she was here, and she forced herself to remember that she was supposed to be seen. The lobby milled with guests of every species, sentry droids, even a few stormtroopers, a few of whom glanced her way. So far, so good.

She approached the wide concierge desk. A bored human woman with premature lines around her eyes forced a smile and said, "How may I help you?"

"I'm here for a meeting," Qi'ra said, chin held high. "Can you direct me to the Obsidian Room?"

The concierge pointed. "Take the glass tram to the penthouse concourse," she directed. "It's at the very top of the hill, the tram's final stop. The Obsidian Room will be down the corridor, beyond the personal residences."

That sounded easy enough. "Thank you," Qi'ra said.

Even though she had only a few minutes left to make the appointment on time, she spent a precious moment to take stock.

Qi'ra always had a backup plan. Always. It had saved her life more than once. So she noted a glass office behind the reception lobby. The desks might provide good cover, if she could get past the sentry droids. To her left was a security booth; everyone milling around had decent armor and well-used blasters, but the uniforms were private sector, not Imperial. Still, she'd have to keep an eye out for them if anything went down. A hallway stretched right, leading to a ballroom, also guarded by sentry droids. Near the back, a sign promised another tram with direct access to the spaceport. Finally, she spotted what she was looking for: a nondescript door with an access panel, partly hidden by a potted plant. A gray-haired woman in a housekeeping uniform approached it and punched in a code. Qi'ra angled herself to watch, memorizing the code.

That was the door she'd use if she needed to make a quick exit. An employee-only corridor was her best chance at finding sewer access without going out the front door and facing those turrets.

Knowledge always made her feel better. Buoyed, Qi'ra turned toward the glass tram the concierge had indicated. Several beings were already inside—two humans, a droid, and a short, hairy alien whose species she'd never encountered before. They all parted to make room, and she pushed the button indicating her destination as the penthouse concourse.

The doors slid closed, and her feet were nearly jerked out from under her as the tram capsule zoomed along the concourse. Qi'ra was supposed to be poised, serene, implacable. But she couldn't help turning to gawk at the sights like an offworld tourist.

The tram skimmed along the outskirts of the Buckell Center, gradually working its way up the hillside, thus offering an unmatched view of the city of Coronet, with its grimy markets and buzzing thoroughfares in the center, the churning factories and shipyards at the edges, and beyond it all the massive spaceport with one of the highest traffic capacities in the galaxy. Qi'ra felt as though she was flying, nothing between her and the Corellian sky but pure air and speed. The city blurred below her—with pollution, with distance, with gloom— but as the tram continued to climb the hill, everything crystalized. The man standing beside her gasped.

They had ascended above the smog line, and the sky was the most glorious cerulean she had ever seen. The smog stretched below them, brownish red and as thick as a blanket. But along the horizon were mountains, actual mountains, tinged green with life and blazing with morning sunshine.

The planet of her birth was beautiful. More beautiful than she'd ever imagined.

The tram made several stops, and passengers trickled in and out. Finally, it glided gently to a halt at the penthouse concourse, and Qi'ra stepped out reluctantly, her eyes still feeling a little glazed. She blinked, took a deep breath, and continued on her way.

The corridor she traveled had regular doorways on either side, just like the tunnel with their bunk cells. But this hallway felt so much longer, the ceiling so much higher, promising a large, comfortable airy space behind each door instead of another dark hole. Every detail, from the lights on the walls to the decorative room numbers, seemed to indicate an impossible excess of wealth.

She was staring at the wall decorations—here, in a hallway, where anyone could just take them!—when a janitor droid scooted past and startled her. She almost squealed, but then she smiled, delighted. She'd always wondered what janitor droids looked like, before they were reengineered to catch rats. It was still a boxy little thing, but sleeker, with cleaning brushes instead of pincers, moving efficiently down the corridor, cleaning up dirt too small for her to notice.

When Qi'ra looked up again, she had reached her destination: the Obsidian Room, a high-security luxury suite for Corellia's finest class of visitor. She raised her hand to the access panel, and the doorway slid open, keyed to her palm. How Lady Proxima had managed to key a distant hotel room to her palm print was too terrifying to contemplate.

She straightened her shoulders and stepped inside.

The living area of the penthouse suite had been cleared of furniture, and her footsteps echoed on marble tile. A vast window looked out on that incredible sky, and it was with some effort that Qi'ra ignored it to size up her situation.

Three others were already in attendance: a small human male with a pointed, ratlike face and a furtive demeanor, a taller middle-aged woman with hulking shoulders and a severe gray bun, and a silver protocol droid with a dented right arm. They all stared as she approached, and she realized, with a sinking heart, that she was the only one who was unarmed.

Come to think of it, she'd never seen a protocol droid carrying weapons before. Strange.

"So nice of you to join us," said the rat-faced man to Qi'ra. "What have you been up to?"

"I've been dusting crops, the easiest job in the galaxy," she replied smoothly.

The rat-faced man nodded. "Then we shall get started right away. We'll begin with the representative of the White Worms. What is your bid, young miss?"

This was the moment she'd been waiting for. Qi'ra raised her head high and said proudly, "The White Worm bid is four hundred and fifty thousand credits."

She couldn't even imagine such a sum. So much money! But she kept her expression cool, as if it were just another day in her life.

The tall woman chuckled. Even the droid gave Qi'ra an odd look. The rat-faced man's hand shifted toward his blaster.

And all of Qi'ra's enthusiasm for this assignment came crashing down. Somehow, her message had been poorly received. She was not a person who was prone to mistakes, but maybe she had forgotten something? Said the wrong thing?

The rat-faced man turned toward the tall woman. "Your turn."

She said, "The Kaldana Syndicate bid is six hundred and seventy-five *million* credits."

Qi'ra had trouble keeping the shock from her face. She had no idea what they were bidding for, but whatever it was, Lady Proxima's bid had been so low as to be insulting.

"And you?" the rat-faced man said, turning to the droid.

"It is my honor and pleasure to inform you that the Droid Gotra bids one billion credits."

The gray-haired woman's dismay was clearly visible. Her fingers twitched near the blaster at her hip.

"Excellent," said the rat-faced man. "One moment as I check with my superiors."

He pulled out a comlink and began speaking in a language Qi'ra couldn't identify. While he spoke, she rehearsed what she'd heard in her head. *The Kaldana Syndicate. The Droid Gotra.* Her bid had been too low, but at least she could return to Lady Proxima with information. Maybe the position of Head was still within reach.

The rat-faced man's eyes grew wide, and he argued back fiercely about something. His hand rested on his blaster. The woman and the droid looked as though they were ready for anything.

At last he stashed his comlink in a pocket. "I'm sorry it had to come to this," he said, and he raised his blaster and pointed it at Qi'ra.

"Wait, wait! I can fix this!" Her hands came up in protest as her mind traveled a thousand meters per second. She knew she couldn't outrun a blaster. So she had to stall, figure a way out of this room.

The rat-faced man did not pull the trigger. He raised an eyebrow, waiting to see what she'd say next.

"Just kill her," the woman said. "She obviously didn't take this seriously. To me that says she's a mole. Maybe CorSec."

"It's clear our bid was insulting," Qi'ra conceded. "But I represent one of Corellia's biggest players. I'm sure I can put in a good word with the White Worms and get a revised bid. I came in good faith, unarmed, see? Would

CorSec have come unarmed?" She hardly had any idea what she was saying; she just knew she had to say something, anything, until she could figure out a plan. There was no furniture in the room. Nothing to hide behind except the droid, and then he might start shooting at her too. No way to get out the door without waiting for the palm scanner to operate. She was stuck in the worst way.

The only other out was that huge window. It was undoubtedly built to withstand extraordinary pressure and winds, even the occasional lightning strike. But maybe a direct hit from a blaster at full power would do the trick. A broken window would create chaos, maybe give her a chance to escape. She had to get someone to shoot at the glass.

The rat-faced man said, "Are you authorized to offer a higher bid?" He raised an eyebrow. "*That* much higher?"

"Yes, of course," Qi'ra said without hesitation. Which was a lie. She had no comlink, no resources, no real power. Still, despite everything, it was a rush to be taken seriously. As if she were an actual player. Someone who could make things happen. Her head felt a little dizzy with it all.

"One moment while I contact my superiors again," he said, and pulled out his comlink.

While the rat-faced man spoke over the comlink, the gray-haired woman glared at Qi'ra and the droid muttered, "Oh, dear. This is not going the way I expected at all. Revised bids! It's all very untoward."

"We should *all* get to revise our bids," the gray-haired woman said. "It's only fair."

The rat-faced man looked up. "My superiors have decided not to accept any revised bids. They are very pleased with the offer presented by the Droid Gotra."

"No!" the gray-haired woman said. "You'd give it to droids over humans?"

Qi'ra logged that bit of information too. The Kaldana Syndicate had also underbid, counting on the seller to show favoritism toward humans.

The rat-faced man ignored her. To the protocol droid, he said, "You may now acquire the merchandise in the agreed upon manner."

It was on the tip of Qi'ra's tongue to inquire if this meant she wasn't going to get shot after all, but the gray-haired woman pulled out her own comlink and angrily informed someone that they had lost the bid.

Qi'ra began backing toward the door.

"Everyone?" the gray-haired woman said into the comlink. "Fine, I understand." And she drew her blaster.

"Watch out!" Qi'ra cried. "The droid is about to shoot!"

The droid was about to do no such thing, but he *was* standing in front of the window. The gray-haired woman reacted with dizzying speed, firing her blaster and nicking his shiny silver shoulder. The majority of the blast crashed into the window glass, causing cracks to spiderweb out from the point of impact.

Qi'ra continued moving toward the doorway while the glass crackled and popped, fissures spreading. Everyone was in motion now. The rat-faced man and the droid fired back at the woman; one of the blasts came so close to Qi'ra's face that she felt heat against her cheek.

She didn't know anything about blasters and fighting, but she'd heard somewhere that moving targets were harder to hit. So she abandoned all subtlety and cartwheeled across the room, barreling toward the door. The window cracks gave, and icy air rushed in hard and fast, lifting her hair, causing her eyes to stream with tears.

Qi'ra palmed the door lock. Another blast ripped into the wall, missing her scalp by millimeters. The door slid open, and she rushed outside, slamming her palm against the lock even as another bolt chased her into the hallway and shattered a mirror hanging on the wall.

The door slid closed. Qi'ra grabbed a potted fern; it was so huge she strained to lift it. She slammed the planter base into the door panel, crushing it to pieces. Then she dropped the plant—it barely missed her foot— and fled down the corridor toward the tram.

Taking the tram was a risk; she knew it even as she

entered. The walls of the entire complex were probably alarmed with sensors. Security personnel already knew there had been a breach. A tram capsule coming from the penthouses would surely attract attention. They might even be waiting for her.

But a complex this size had multiple trams and corridors. Security couldn't possibly cover them all, not even with all the security droids she'd seen. She'd get her best odds of survival by taking the fastest way back.

Just in case, though, she punched the dining concourse as her destination rather than the lobby; it wouldn't do to exit right in front of that security booth. She'd depend on the tram to get her most of the way and figure it out from there.

She was the only passenger this time—a small bit of luck. But her minor celebration was short-lived when the tram stopped at concourse three to pick up another passenger, and again at concourse two, where a whole family of tentacle-faced Quarren stepped inside. Just as well. Maybe it would be easier to blend into a crowd.

Finally, the elevator reached the dining court. She breathed relief when the door slid open and no one was there to greet her with blasters. Qi'ra and the Quarren family stepped out. She strode forward with purpose, as though she knew exactly where she was going, but all the while she was taking in tiny details, anything that might help.

This area contained several restaurants, a designer jewelry shop, a high-end salon, and access to a massive indoor bathing pool. She headed toward one of the restaurants, for no other reason than it seemed the busiest—a dark candlelit place filled with stone columns and lush plants that promised authentic Alderaanian cuisine.

Qi'ra stopped just outside and pretended to peruse the posted menu, but her mind was whirring with possibilities. A grand staircase to her left curved downward. Maybe she could wait for a large group of people to descend and try to blend in with them. If only Lady Proxima had thought to give her a little money. The Buckell Center boasted several taxi stands; it would have been the easiest thing in the world to hire a speeder cab.

She could steal some money. Qi'ra had stolen a few times for Lady Proxima; it wasn't so hard. And if she felt bad for the people she stole from, she didn't let it get to her. Anything was worth survival.

Qi'ra scanned the crowd for a likely mark. She preferred coins to credit chips, as the former were completely untraceable, but she knew her chances of finding any were low. With the Imperial presence so strong here, any currency besides Imperial credits was strongly discouraged.

A siren wailed. Everyone in the Alderaanian restaurant paused what they were doing and glanced around, trying to figure out what was going on.

Qi'ra knew exactly what was going on, and her window of time for sneaking away clean was getting smaller and smaller. At some point soon, she might have to abandon strategic moves in favor of running for her life.

A man in long robes strode past. A bulge at his waist indicated some sort of pouch tucked under his utility belt. Qi'ra moved to follow.

She stayed several steps behind as he plunged down the corridor. The robed man turned right into a long hallway and nearly collided with a group of guards— four of them running in formation, blasters held at the ready. Qi'ra almost turned and fled, but they ran right past her.

Which meant they weren't specifically looking for her. At least not yet.

Qi'ra continued to follow the robed man, hoping an opportunity would present itself soon. She just needed to get him alone. Her pickpocketing skills were serviceable, but she was no Jagleo. That White Worm girl could shave a Wookiee bald without being caught.

The man slowed as he neared a hotel room door, pulling out a key card. Qi'ra began to reach for his pouch.

A siren wailed again, louder. The man spun in alarm, noticing Qi'ra for the first time. She quickly dropped her hand. The two stared at each other a moment.

"What a distressing sound!" Qi'ra said with a smile. She took a few steps past him, as if she had been going that direction anyway, but she silently cursed her bad luck.

The man stepped inside his room, and the door closed behind him. Qi'ra had wasted precious minutes following him. Now she had to start over with another mark.

More running footsteps. Qi'ra faced a doorway and pretended to search for a keycard as another group of armed guards dashed by.

She caught the tail end of a comlink conversation. "A young human female," said a male voice. "Brown, chin-length hair, barely more than one and a half meters tall. Wanted immediately for questioning."

Even after the guards passed and the sounds of their footsteps faded, Qi'ra remained in the doorway, collecting herself. Her heart was racing, her breath coming too fast. She felt a storm front of panic approaching, like a darkness that clouded her thoughts.

No, she was not a panicker. She would be calm. She would be poised. She would *think*.

They were looking for her specifically now, which meant there was no time to find another mark, pick a pocket, and hire a speeder cab. She had to reach the lobby and find the access door she'd spotted earlier, the one that might lead to the sewers. And if she couldn't do it in stealth, then she would just have to run for it.

Calmly, she continued down the hallway, looking for a lift or stairwell.

She found something even better: Another off-limits door, just like the one she'd spotted earlier, with an access pad.

Qi'ra took a deep breath, unsure if she remembered the code she'd observed earlier. Praying to every god she'd ever heard of that she would remember correctly—and that the code would be the same here as in the lobby—she punched it in.

Nothing happened.

Qi'ra was about to try again when the ambient music in the hallway went silent; she hadn't even realized it was playing until it was suddenly gone.

Speakers crackled. A voice boomed overhead, undoubtedly broadcast complex-wide.

"This is Senior Manager Ellias Gorlin asking everyone to please stay calm. Due to a minor environmental breach in one of our penthouse units, the Buckell Center is under complete lockdown until further notice. In

gratitude for your patience and understanding, all ame-
nities, including spa services, restaurants, holovids, and
fine shopping, will be offered at a ten percent discount.
We will let you know as soon as it is safe for anyone to
enter or leave the center. Please enjoy the rest of your day."

Qi'ra felt the edge of panic creeping back. The entire
complex under lockdown because of a breach in one
room? Not likely. A lockdown reeked of Imperial entan-
glement, which was so far above her pay grade it made
her head spin.

When she'd escaped the Obsidian Room, everyone
had been shooting at each other. She wouldn't be surprised to learn that they were all dead, trapped by the
door she'd purposely jammed. What if someone inside
was even more important than she realized? Or maybe it
was the deal itself that had attracted Imperial attention.
That droid had bid a billion credits!

Whatever the cause, one thing was sure: there was
no way she was getting past those defensive turrets out
front. She either had to reach the sewer access or find a
place in the complex to hunker down until they gave up
searching for her.

Qi'ra stared down at the access panel. Maybe she had
remembered the code incorrectly. She closed her eyes,
trying to put herself back in the moment. The woman
had been wearing a service uniform. The air had smelled

like the vine lilies climbing up the massive center trellis, and it had been a little damp from the indoor water-fall. Qi'ra had shifted to the left to get a better view; the woman's fingers had moved . . .

That was it. Qi'ra saw it clear as day. She had gotten one digit wrong.

She punched in the correct code. The access lights turned blue, and the door slid open, revealing a narrow, dim corridor stripped of luxury and flowery scent.

Qi'ra nearly sobbed with relief. She ducked inside and pressed against the wall while the door slid shut behind her.

Now all she had to do was find a service lift and a basement. Every major building in Coronet was accessible by sewer and maintenance tunnels, and as one of Lady Proxima's most trusted scrumrats, she had secret access to almost all of them. She'd have to watch for traps, sentries, and management droids, sure. Full lockdown meant that even a sewer entrance might be guarded. But she had a chance now. She was smart and resourceful, and she could do this.

Qi'ra moved forward at a jog, already rehearsing a story for why she was in the corridor, just in case she ran into someone.

CHAPTER 3

Han had barely made it into the sewer tunnel before a ratcatcher droid collided with his ankle. He looked down. Sure enough, the panel light was glowing a steady red. Lady Proxima and her lieutenants thought a steady red light on a ratcatcher droid meant it needed to be recharged, but Han knew better. It really meant that the droid contained a message.

With Tsuulo's help, the White Worm kids had been using ratcatcher droids to exchange information, even small items. Lady Proxima was sure to find out about it eventually; Han didn't know what would happen to the little droids then. But for now, it remained the safest way to communicate with each other under her nose.

He bent down and opened the rat compartment. Inside was a dog biscuit.

Han laughed out loud before he could stop himself. The biscuit was about the size of his palm and as hard as a mud brick, and Han knew it would taste faintly of fish. It was one of the "treats" Rebolt gave his massive drooling hounds. Tsuulo must have swiped it from the kennels, knowing Han would get hungry after not finishing a full breakfast.

Dog biscuits weren't exactly luxury fare, but they were nutritious and edible to most bipedal species, and Han was grateful to have one. He shoved it into his pocket and proceeded down the tunnel.

His route would take him near Old Man Powlo's territory again, but thankfully not through it. Then again, the weight of the dog biscuit in his pocket gave him an idea.

He would have to hurry to pull it off and still make his mysterious appointment at the Foundry, so he hastened into a jog, splashing through the tunnel without regard for stealth and caution. Plenty of time for that later, right?

He turned into the warren of darker, older tunnels that marked Powlo's territory and found the cave-like lair with ease. The room still glowed, though the fire in the pit had burned down quite a bit. Powlo lay on his side facing the entrance, on a pallet made of rags and rat skins and rotting underbrush. His eyes were closed, his breathing steady and even.

Han cleared his throat.

Powlo cracked one eye open, then the other. He sneer-grinned and said, "Han. Friend."

"Yep, that's me," Han said. "Here, I brought you something." He reached into his pocket and grabbed the biscuit. He was about to hand over the whole thing, but common sense got the better of him, so he broke the biscuit in two and shoved one half back into his pocket. He would need it later, no doubt about it.

He extended the other half to Powlo. "It's a, uh, treat," he said.

"Treat?"

"Yeah. For eating." Han pantomimed putting the piece of biscuit into his mouth.

Powlo's face brightened, his eyes flashing molten gold. He rose from his pallet and approached, hunch-shouldered and cautious. Then, quicker than a striking snake, he snatched the biscuit from Han's hand and shoved it into his mouth.

"Mmmm, is good," he said, crumbs sticking to the corners of his mouth. The two of them were close now, only a meter apart. Powlo's skin was dry and cracked, and a few wisps of facial hair grew from his chin. What struck Han most, though, was the obvious intelligence in the creature's golden gaze.

Powlo clearly struggled with Galactic Basic, and Han wondered what the fellow's native language was. He had learned a long time before, though, that broken speech almost never indicated lack of intelligence. In fact, he himself probably sounded just like Powlo every time he tried to speak Huttese or Shyriiwook.

"Glad you like it," Han said. "I'll bring more if I can get some. Anyway, I have to go. See you later, Powlo."

Lately, Han's instincts had been telling him to cultivate allies. Maybe it was the fact that Lady Proxima had been even more secretive than usual these past few weeks. Or maybe he was looking for every possible advantage as he leveraged himself for the position of Head. Whatever the case, Han had been making a point of getting to know someone wherever he went, whether it was a cantina, a factory, or even a sewer. It paid to have friends. It especially paid to be owed favors.

That didn't mean he wanted to be soul mates with anyone; Han was a loner, and that suited him just fine. And it didn't mean he *trusted* any of his friends. So as Powlo happily chewed his dog biscuit, Han cautiously backed away, a careful smile on his face.

Powlo didn't bother swallowing before opening his mouth to say, "Bye, Han! See soon!"

"Yeah, see you soon." The moment he was out of sight, Han turned and fled.

As he pushed through the low tunnels, it occurred to him to wonder: What if Powlo hadn't liked the biscuit? Would he have become hostile? Some aliens considered gift giving to be offensive. And some couldn't eat the same food as humans. There were so many ways that could have gone wrong.

Maybe one day, Han should learn to think things through a little better. Then again, where would the fun be in that?

The Foundry was a good hike away, so Han had to hurry. As soon as he reached a larger corridor with room to stand up straight, he sped back up into a jog. It would be a lot faster if he could take the streets, maybe hail a speeder cab. But Lady Proxima was stingy with money, and she hated to run up costs, no matter how important an operation was.

Faintly, through mortar and metal and stone, came the sound of chimes. The Temple of the True Vine was sounding its call to morning prayer. That meant he had minutes to reach the Foundry.

Han burst into an all-out sprint.

The entrance to the Foundry basement was just like the manual airlock of a low-end freighter—a large round portal opened by cranking a wheel. Han suspected that an airtight entrance meant these tunnels could be flooded at a moment's notice. It was a smart precaution, and one he'd have to keep in mind.

Lady Proxima had specifically told him he was not to be seen entering or leaving the Foundry, and he'd been careful while traveling the sewers. But there was no way into the basement except through that hatch. Which was bound to be noisy.

No help for it. Han grabbed the wheel and cranked.

It squealed like an angry Gungan baby, a piercing wail that Han was sure could be heard for kilometers in every direction. He cranked and cranked; the airlock squealed and squealed.

Finally, it popped open. Han scooted inside and pulled the hatch closed behind him. He started to crank the inner wheel to lock it into place, but he thought better of it. Best to leave himself a quick way out.

He half expected his contact to be waiting right there, but the corridor was empty. His footsteps echoed through the tunnel.

He hurried around a corner and jerked to a stop as a huge shadow loomed before him.

"Han," said the shadow in a voice completely devoid of inflection.

Relief flooded through him. It was one of the many contacts he'd been cultivating: TD-H4, a massive, hulking Tool-and-Die series droid. He was a huge steel beast fitted with "arms" that were actually long gadgets: a lathe, a welder, a drill, and even a miniature stamping press. He was mostly obsolete now, but he'd somehow avoided being thrown into the smelter by doing odd jobs for the Foundry, even pulling the occasional sentry shift. Han didn't know how old he was—possibly centuries. In any case, the droid obviously had a knack for survival, and Han couldn't help admiring him.

"Hey, Tool." Han looked past the droid to see if his contact was close by. "It's nice to see you. Look, I'm really sorry, but I don't have any lubricant with me today. I'll try to bring some next time."

Tool waved his welder in dismissal. "Don't worry about it. There are bigger matters at hand today."

"That's great, Tool," Han said, giving the droid a pat on the shoulder, already on his way around Tool when something in his voice made Han stop. The droid's flat tone always made him sound surly to Han's ear, though in all fairness he'd been programmed during an earlier industrial era, before technological advances in vocal intonation or lightweight polymer alloys. "Wait, what did you say?"

"I admit, I'm surprised to see you. I thought this deal would be too big a fish for Lady Proxima's little pond."

Han stared up at him. *Tool* was his contact.

"Did I say something wrong," Tool asked flatly.

"No. It's just . . . you use words like no droid I've ever heard. It's so . . . human."

"Thank you," Tool said. "I adopted some language programming that allows me to make metaphors in Galactic Basic. Follow me, please."

"Huh," Han said, falling in behind the droid. "Well, the language program is definitely working." That was Tool for you, always improving himself. Like the time he'd paid Han to find three very specific screws that he had used to rearticulate the "elbow" joint of his ungainly lathe attachment.

They reached a stairway. Tool struggled to navigate it; his massive knees did not bend easily, and the going was slow.

"Any idea what's going on?" Han asked.

"Yes," Tool said.

"Well, are you going to tell me?"

"You mean you do not know."

"Proxima told me almost nothing."

"That was probably wise."

Han glared at his friend. "Listen, Tool—"

"Everyone in that room thinks my name is Die."

"Huh? I thought it was Teedee-Aychfor. I just call you Tool because—"

"Because I am a huge tool. Yes, I know. Ha-ha. Ha-ha-ha-ha. Thanks to my new language programming, I now understand the jest. You can call me Tool if you like, but I'm going by Die now. I thought it appropriate, given my new position."

"What position? Tool, did you get a job? That's great. I'm real glad for you. What are you—"

They had reached the top of the stairway, and Tool keyed the door open. It slid wide to reveal a bunker-like room, reinforced with cement and durasteel beam construction, all coated with some kind of gray resin. Weak light flickered overhead, illuminating a single conference table made of dull metal, surrounded by bent metal chairs. The scents of rust and mold and dirty grease made Han wrinkle his nose.

Like Tool, the materials in this room were obsolete, holdovers from an earlier industrial era. But if you needed a quiet, unobserved place to make a deal, someone had jury-rigged this underground bunker to do the trick just fine. It wouldn't surprise Han to learn the walls were a meter thick, or that the resin coating blocked heat sensors and was waterproof. Where innovation was high but resources were low, you took what you had, slapped it all together, and hoped it held. It was the Corellian way.

Two people, both humans, were already sitting at the table, and they looked up as Han and Tool entered. One was a dark-skinned male with the most ridiculous mustache Han had ever seen—thick and fuzzy as a caterpillar, except with waxed points on either end that drooped all the way past the fellow's jowls to his jawline.

The other was a pale brunet woman with gray at her temples. She wore all black, including a flight jacket.

The only splash of color was a patch on the upper arm of her jacket—a bright yellow triangle with concave sides. The insignia marked her as Kaldana Syndicate.

Han usually tried to avoid the Kaldana. They were serious business.

The man with the ridiculous mustache said, "Hello, young man. What have you been up to?"

"Uh . . . Oh, right. I've been dusting crops, the easiest job in the galaxy."

The man's mustache twitched. "And your name?"

"Han."

"Han what?"

"Han nothing. Just Han."

"And who are you representing today?"

"Uh . . . the White Worms?"

"Excellent. Please have a seat, Han Nothing of the White Worms."

Han pulled back a chair and sat. As he did, he noticed that both the mustached fellow and the Kaldana woman wore enormous holsters. Han didn't know much about blasters, but based on the size of those holsters, they were packing a lot of firepower. Lady Proxima had never given him more than a knife, and this time she hadn't even given him that. Although he supposed there was no point bringing a knife to a gun fight.

"And of course we are already acquainted with Die," Mustache Guy continued. "Thank you for representing the Droid Gotra today. We will understand if you are anatomically incapable of"—he waved a dismissive hand— "performing a sitting gesture."

Han wasn't sure how he knew, but he was certain that last bit was meant as an insult to his friend Tool. If his hackles weren't already up from being in a secure bunker with two well-armed strangers, they were now. And Tool wasn't his contact; the droid was another messenger, like him.

The three humans faced each other at the table, and Tool loomed over Han's shoulder. Han waited for someone to say something, but everyone seemed content with silence.

"So . . ." Han said. "Anybody here play sabacc? I didn't bring a deck with me, but if any of you happen to have one . . ."

The Kaldana woman raised an eyebrow but said nothing. The mustached man just stared off into space.

They were waiting for something, and Han had no idea what. He could ask, but he had a funny feeling that revealing his ignorance would be a bad move. He'd have to play it cool.

He leaned back in his chair, trying to act casual. "It's a great morning for making a deal," he said, and as soon as the words were out of his mouth, he knew he sounded like a dumb kid who was trying too hard.

Han decided to use a different approach. "Neither of you told me your name," he said.

Still nothing, unless you counted the exasperated look from the Kaldana woman.

The Kaldana. Here in the Foundry basement, no less. To the best of Han's knowledge, they were an organization of pirates and shipjackers, formed to take advantage of the inevitable smuggling traffic in Corellian skies. Now that the Empire had a stranglehold on shipbuilding, anyone else who wanted components had to get them out the hard way, and the Kaldana were always lying in wait, hoping for an easy score. Their interests sometimes took them planetside, and the White Worms had encountered them occasionally in the streets. But never below ground. Corellia's criminal organizations generally gave each other space, and everyone knew that the dark underbelly of Coronet was Lady Proxima's territory. Something serious must be going down for the Kaldana to conduct business here—and for Proxima to let them.

Han looked up at his friend Tool. Mustache Guy had said he was representing something called the Droid Gouda or Grotto or something like that. Whatever it was, Han had never heard of it. He wouldn't be surprised if

Tsuulo or Qi'ra knew, though. Maybe he'd make a point to ask one of them when he got back to the White Worm lair.

Thinking of Qi'ra made him wonder about her errand. Odd that Proxima would give two of her oldest scrumrats tasks the same morning. Her gang was a nighttime organization, with few exceptions.

Obviously, their two errands were related somehow. When they got back to the lair, maybe he could convince Qi'ra that it was in both of their best interests to trade information, see what they could learn from each other.

The moments ticked by. Han realized he was bouncing his leg under the table and forced himself to be still. Overhead, the lights buzzed and flickered.

He nearly jumped out of his chair when someone's comlink pinged.

Mustache Guy pulled his from his pocket and listened. Han strained to hear but couldn't pick up the other half of the conversation at all.

"Understood," Mustache Guy said. "Yes, I can handle it." He stashed his comlink, then rose to his feet.

"Well?" the Kaldana woman asked.

"The winning bid was submitted by the Droid Gotra," he said.

The woman gasped.

"Apparently, the White Worms weren't even in the running," Mustache Guy continued. "An embarrassment for them, really."

Han had no idea what that meant, but he was sure it was nothing good.

Tool stepped forward, and one of his massive legs accidentally banged an empty chair, toppling it. "In that case may I see the merchandise please," he intoned.

"Of course," Mustache Guy said, reaching into his pocket again.

"Wait!" said the woman. "Surely there's been some mistake? My organization put together an impressive bid. I don't understand how—"

"The Gotra's bid was the *most* impressive," Mustache Guy assured her. "I'm sorry, but you lost."

The woman's hand twitched toward her blaster holster as her eyes darted back and forth between Mustache Guy and Tool.

Han considered fleeing. The White Worms had lost some kind of auction, that much was clear. There was no sense hanging around. Proxima had promised him the Head position if things went well; surely this constituted things *not* going well? Not that he'd had any control over the outcome at all. It was just that he trusted Lady Proxima about as much as he trusted the good will of a CorSec officer. He couldn't count on her to play fair.

But maybe if he stuck around, gathered some information, he could redeem himself in her eyes. It was his only chance. He stayed put.

Mustache Guy pulled out a tiny hinged chest, engraved with vines and flowers. It was only about a fourth the size of a ratcatcher droid.

"Is that it?" the woman asked, leaning forward.

"No. The Droid Gotra's merchandise is inside." He fiddled with it, pressing a flower petal here, a hinge there. It was a puzzle box, Han realized. Meant to hide something of incredible worth. Jewelry? Credit chips? Precious stones?

Something hissed, and the lid popped up on its hinge, revealing a red velvet pillow. Pressed into the pillow was a shiny datacube.

A compartment in Tool's chest swung open, and he extended a long pincer, grabbing the cube. "A pleasure doing business with you," he said in his flat voice. "Or do I have that backwards. I also understand that business always comes before pleasure. . . ."

Han stood to leave, not sure he had gleaned any information of note. That the Droid Gorda had won an auction for a datacube? That the Kaldana representative was angry as hell? Han felt more confused than ever. "I guess I'll be going," he said. "Congratulations . . . Die."

Just as he turned to go, the door leading to the

Foundry flew open, and six men burst through, all wearing black.

Han ducked under the table, but not before he noticed their Kaldana triangle insignias and their giant blasters.

"Up against the wall!" someone yelled. "All of you."

Han remained crouched for the space of several heartbeats. Was he fast enough to make it into the stairwell before blasters started firing? Probably not.

Resigned, he gradually rose from the ground, hands in the air. "Surely we can talk this out?" he said. "I'm just a—"

"Shut up," said one of the men. "Against the wall. Now." He waved his blaster at Han.

Han complied, but he placed himself as close to the stairwell as possible. Mustache Guy's back was already pressed as far into the wall as it could go, as if the fellow was hoping he'd sink right in and disappear. Tool was beside him, the datacube still held in his pincer.

The Kaldana woman, on the other hand, had moved to stand with her fellow thugs, a smug grin on her face. "Hand over the datacube," she said to Tool. "If you do, no one gets hurt. Not that a droid cares about humans."

"He looks to be a century old, at least," said one of the thugs.

"Older," said another. "Should have been sent to the scrap heap a long time ago."

"Well, it's never too late to right a wrong," said the first guy, and he aimed his blaster at Tool's head.

"Wait," said Tool. "I'll hand it over." But then Han heard, clear as day even though it was barely more than a whisper: "Get ready, Han."

Ready for what? he almost asked, even as he groped with the realization that Tool had modulated his voice so that only Han could hear him.

Tool stepped forward, putting his hulking metal frame between Han and the Kaldana blasters. Han crept toward the door.

"I'm so sorry it had to come to this," Tool said to the thugs, "but I'm a fly caught in your trap. Or would it be better to say web. In any case I'm in a snare. Like a caught fly."

Was Tool stalling? Han was almost to the door now.

With mind-numbing speed, Tool twisted on the axis of his waist, pivoting a full one hundred eighty degrees. "Han, catch," he said, and tossed the data cube to him.

Han was reaching for it, snatching it from the air, before his mind registered what was happening.

Tool lurched toward him; blaster fire had caught him in the back. "Now run," Tool said blandly, as if nothing was happening. "For your life. I will make a stand here. Do not let that datacube out of your sight. No matter what."

Han was already fiddling with the door. It slid open as more blaster fire erupted against Tool's flank. How was he withstanding all this?

Every single attachment Tool had ever been fitted with popped out of his carapace. His lathe began whirling, and his welder lit up with blue fire as he stepped away from Han, advancing toward his Kaldana foes. "Run," he commanded again, and this time his voice was as loud as thunder.

The sounds of whining machinery and gunfire soon mixed with screams.

Han ran, clutching the datacube tight in his fist. Down the staircase he fled, through the airlock door, into the sewer. Blaster fire grew quieter, at first with distance and then with cessation.

His breath came in gasps as he ran as fast as he could. He needed to get back to the lair. He needed to tell Proxima . . . No. His gut instinct told him that was the wrong move. The deal had gone badly, and it would be just like her to sacrifice a scrumrat to save face and curry favor with the Kaldana. Better that than an all-out gang war. If he returned now, his life would be forfeit.

He stopped in his tracks. What should he do? Where could he go? He stared at the datacube in his hand. All this trouble for something so tiny. Whatever information it contained was worth killing for.

Or dying for. Tool was probably a heap of scrap now. He had sacrificed himself for Han. Or maybe for the data this cube contained. Han hadn't realized a droid was capable of such an act.

Maybe he shouldn't count his friend out yet. The way he'd withstood that blaster fire . . . Han wouldn't have believed it if he hadn't seen it himself. Maybe Tool was made of something even stronger than steel. Maybe all those self-modifications had paid off. Which meant there was still hope.

A skittering noise put him on high alert. A moment later, a dozen rats blurred past him; one bold fellow clambered right over his boot.

He was used to rats; they didn't scare him. But he was definitely scared of whatever had scared *them*. Han stilled himself, held his breath, and listened.

Sure enough, footsteps sounded. Faint splashing. An angry yell. The noise was echoing and distant, but coming closer. Tool's sacrifice had bought time but not victory. The Kaldana were in pursuit.

Han ran as fast as he'd ever run in his life, away from the sewer tunnels that led back to the White Worm den, heading toward the center of town instead. Low-hanging pipes and cracks in the floor and even the occasional sewage block all conspired to slow him down, but he kept alert, dodging and jumping and pumping his legs as fast as he could.

He had no idea where he was going or what he would do next. But he figured that gave him the advantage, since the Kaldana killers had no idea either. He'd have to figure out his strategy along the way. For now, he just had to evade his pursuers and count on his luck to hold.

CHAPTER 4

Qi'ra found a laundry station in the basement of the Buckell Center, filled with huge vats steaming with pungent cleaner, staffed by worker droids. Ignoring the droids, she followed the water pipes until she discovered where they dumped out: a massive grate in the floor.

Just as she was lifting the grate, sentry droids poured into the laundry station. Qi'ra had no choice but to plunge through the hole.

Thankfully, she didn't have far to drop. She splash-landed in an underground basin. The water was less than a meter deep—just enough to break her fall—but the bottom was slick with algae and sewage, and the surface held an oily sheen from the laundry cleaning agent. Her beautiful new skirt was ruined.

Fortunately, the droids couldn't follow; they were a standard-issue security series, not equipped for aquatic maneuvers. It meant she had a little time before their superiors sent someone after her who was better outfitted.

Probably a *very* little time. Just enough to catch her breath and make a plan.

She had to get back to Lady Proxima in the White
Worm den. She had valuable information: the identities
of the other bidders, for instance. Surely that was worth
something?

Qi'ra had far exceeded the scope of her authority for
this assignment by pretending she could revise their bid.
As if she had any negotiating power, or spoke for Lady
Proxima in some way. There might be hell to pay if the
White Worm leader learned of it. Especially if that was
what had set off the shooting spree upstairs.

She pushed forward, thigh-deep in murky water,
thinking as she went. If *she* were Lady Proxima, she'd
appreciate having an underling with some initiative. In
fact, if she ever ended up in a position of authority over
others, she'd be sure to cultivate those like her. People
who could think strategically on their feet, for the good
of the organization.

Something tugged at her hip and she reacted too fast,
jerking free and tearing her skirt. She stumbled forward, sloshing water onto her beautiful red shirt. She
lifted her hem out of the water and saw that she'd torn
the bottom on some stray scrap of metal. What a waste.

Shoving regret aside, she pushed forward through
the filthy water, making sure to stay away from the edges.

If she ended up in a position of authority someday,
she'd never have to wade through sewer muck again.

She'd have scrumrats who could do it for her. Everything about that complex had been so beautiful. So elegant. So *clean*. It was a place that *felt* right with its open air, room to breathe, people who listened to her. If only she could have sped off in a cab, or flown away in a ship. Anything but go crashing back to the dark, filthy sewers.

Qi'ra reached the edge of the basin. Three storm tunnels gaped open in the wall before her, set all in a row. The one on the right took a hard turn back toward central Coronet, so that wasn't an option. The other two would get her nearer the White Worm lair, and though the leftmost tunnel would force her to take a longer route, it would also provide more twists and turns.

Either of them would be safe enough, as long as it didn't start raining.

She wasted precious moments debating between the two tunnels. Light flashed in the middle one, followed by a clunking sound.

Something or someone was coming toward her.

She reached down and ripped the torn piece of fabric from her skirt. Then she tossed it onto the edge of the right tunnel, where it was sure to be noticed, before launching herself into the one on the left. She bruised her shin in her haste to climb up. It was too low to run; she half crouched, half crawled as she pushed forward into darkness.

The decoy fabric might buy her only a minute or two.

Lady Proxima would protect her. It was the only rational thing for her to do. Qi'ra was one of her most valuable scrumrats, or she wouldn't have been sent on this mission in the first place. Moloch and the other lieutenants could hold off any pursuers. Even that idiot Rebolt and his hounds could be formidable in a pinch. She just had to get there.

Footsteps and splashing echoed behind her. It sounded like a whole army was coming. "This way!" a man called. "Someone entered this tunnel recently!"

Blast. Her decoy hadn't worked. At the very least, she'd been hoping they'd split up, unsure which way she went.

She knew better than to count on luck, though. That's why she always had a plan, and her plan was to reach the warren of the Old Town sewers. There were so many intersections and dead ends, and she knew every single one. She could easily lose her pursuers there. So long as she didn't panic. So long as she was smart, quiet, and fast.

The tunnel opened up, and her back and shoulders thanked her for the opportunity to stand up straight. Light poured down from a storm drain above her head. To her left was another tunnel, sloped slightly upward. It was a tough, slippery climb through sewer muck, but if she made it, she'd have a real chance.

She plunged in and used forearms, elbows, and knees to leverage herself upward. Water ran past her in the other direction. It was almost nothing, the merest trickle, but it was just enough to make the tunnel floor slick and hard to navigate.

"Which way did she go?" boomed a voice, and Qi'ra froze. Sound was tricky in these tunnels. Sometimes a noise as loud as a freighter engine was really a kilometer away. And sometimes the merest whisper of sound was as close as your ear.

"I think she's headed toward Old Town," someone else said.

"Call dispatch. Tell them to send a unit to Old Town to cut her off."

"Yes, sir."

Qi'ra crept forward silently. Stealth was more important than speed in this slick, upward-sloping tunnel. Otherwise she'd lose her feet and slide right back into the arms of those CorSec guards.

Every bit of forward progress was agony. Her heart was too loud in her chest, and her breath came fast and hard. A lip of darkness lay ahead. She just had to reach it.

Lights flashed against the walls around her, turning them from gray black to rust red.

"Hey, I think I see her! Stop right there or I'll shoot. . . ."

Qi'ra heaved herself up over the lip of darkness onto a stone ledge. No time to rest or even think, because guards were climbing up the tunnel after her.

She hopped to her feet and plunged forward at a dead run, counting on the darkness to keep her safe from blaster fire. Ahead was a branching corridor that ran beneath an old cantina. Qi'ra didn't know who owned the cantina or exactly what went on in that less-than-fine establishment, but she did know that sometimes they had to dump product fast, and they'd built a chute for exactly that purpose.

All the White Worm scrumrats knew about it. Occasionally, Lady Proxima was paid by the cantina owner to retrieve the product—usually nothing more than shipyard components, but sometimes money or even spice. In return, the White Worms got to use the chute whenever they needed to evade pursuers. It was a mutually beneficial arrangement, and it would be Qi'ra's salvation.

She reached the corridor and paused to listen. The guards had said something about cutting her off in Old Town, so there was always the chance that someone would be waiting to intercept her.

All was quiet, save for a steady, echoing *drip-drip-plop*. She plunged inside.

Something exploded on the ledge she'd just vacated.

Qi'ra tumbled to her knees, holding her hands to her

ears. It took a moment to realize what had happened. Not a real explosion. Someone had thrown a stun charge. If she hadn't turned inside the corridor when she did, she'd be flat on her back, probably unconscious.

She scrambled to her feet and sprinted ahead, but her gait was unsteady, her ears ringing. Just a little farther . . . There! She saw the chute. It was covered by a curtain of sorts, a burlap-like material painted to blend in with the wall around it. Once inside, she would slide right into White Worm territory.

Footsteps splashed nearby—too near. She reached for the curtain.

Someone barreled into her, sending her sprawling in the muck. Hands were reaching for her. She fought back like a rancor, attacking blindly with hands and feet. "Get off of—" she started to yell.

"Qi'ra!" said a familiar voice. "It's me. C'mon, we have to get out of here."

Hands reached for her again.

"Han?"

"People are after me. You can't stay here."

"After *you*?" Qi'ra threw off his hands and scrambled to her feet on her own.

"Come *on!*" He tried to pull her back, away from the entrance to the chute.

"Han, what are you doing?" Why did he keep grabbing

her? The guards would be on them at any moment. "The chute is right there! We could be back at Proxima's in less than—"

"We're not going back there." Her heels made furrows in sewer mud as he dragged her away.

"But I have a plan—"

Another stun charge lit up the tunnel, turning Qi'ra's sight into fire, her hearing into clanging cymbals. "Blast," she said through it all. "They cut me off."

There was no reaching the chute now. It was too late. Han had ruined everything, and now they were probably going to die.

"Please, Qi'ra," Han said. "I don't want to leave you behind."

She had no choice but to follow him. It was the only way left not blocked by guards and stun charges.

Together, they plunged into the dark, footsteps close at their heels.

CHAPTER 5

They reached an intersection.

"Go left," Qi'ra said.

Han grabbed her arm and pulled her into the corridor on the right.

"What are you doing? I said to go left!"

"Trust me."

Their breath was coming in gasps as they ran, making it hard to talk.

"You have a plan?"

"No."

"Then why—"

"Call it a gut feeling."

Qi'ra was so angry she could hardly see straight. At her earliest opportunity, she was going to ditch this loser and get back to the White Worm lair on her own. Leave Han to the guards. Or better yet, force him to come with her so she could smack him in the face herself.

She had been almost safe, almost home, and he had ruined everything.

"At least tell me where we're going."

"How should I know?"

Unbelievable. "You mean you dragged me away from safety, and you didn't even know where you were going?"

"Safety? You're kidding me, right? You head back to the White Worms now and you're dead inside a minute."

"Not a chance. We're valuable to Lady Proxima. We're her top finalists for the position of Head!"

"We're expendable. What do you think happened to the last Head?"

She had no answer for that. No one knew for sure, but they'd all heard the murmurings. The last one, a Grindalid male named Jabbat, had disappeared under mysterious circumstances, in the territory of a fellow everyone called Old Man Powlo. Rumor was that Proxima had dumped his body there on purpose, served him right up to Powlo as part of a deal.

"Proxima doesn't care about you," Han went on relentlessly. "Or me. Or anyone but herself. You know it as well as I do."

Qi'ra was sucking in breath, and her legs burned. She and Han were both slowing down. They couldn't run forever. The weight of exhaustion dragged at her. And maybe the weight of truth. Han was right. Gut feeling or no, he was actually making sense.

"You're right," she admitted.

"I am?"

"About Lady Proxima, anyway."

They were silent for a moment as they concentrated on running. They made a couple of turns that took them south of the White Worm den.

"Look," he said, "if you really want to go back there, I won't get in your way. And I'm sorry I . . . forced things back there. It's just . . . I didn't want . . . Eh, never mind."

That was Han for you. Not so good at expressing himself when it mattered. His reports to Lady Proxima, for instance, were notoriously inept.

"We have to find a place to lay low," she said.

"Agreed."

Well, that was a start. "I have a . . ." Qi'ra stopped herself. Exhaustion and hunger must have been getting to her, because she'd almost confessed her deepest secret. "I know the White Worms keep a few safe houses throughout the city," she said instead.

"I'm not sure a White Worm safe house is a good idea," Han said.

"Why not?"

"Doesn't feel right."

Qi'ra reached out and grabbed his arm, stopping him in his tracks. "Give me facts, Han. *Reasons.*"

The look he gave her could peel the segments from a Grindalid. "Facts just get in the way."

"Do you have a better idea?"

"Yeah, actually. I know a place." He seemed a little stunned, as if the idea had just occurred to him.

"Then lead the way. Fast. I've got Buckell Center guards and CorSec after me."

Han took off at a jog, and Qi'ra followed. "And I've got Kaldana Syndicate killers after me," he said.

"What? Kaldana? I just met with one—"

"Less talking, more running," he said over his shoulder.

Their intimate knowledge of the sewers had helped put distance between them and their pursuers, but it wasn't enough. So Qi'ra concentrated on running without tripping over sewer refuse. They'd talk it all out later, when they were safe.

Han led them through Old Town, and Qi'ra was surprised to recognize some tunnels bordering White Worm territory. They were very close to the lair.

She knew she shouldn't talk—White Worm lookouts could be anywhere in this area—but she couldn't help saying: "I thought you said we shouldn't go back to Proxima's territory!"

"We're not. We're going near it. A place they'll never look."

Something caught Qi'ra's attention: the barest hint of sound.

She grabbed Han and yanked him into a branching tunnel.

"What—" he started to say, but she shushed him.

The sound came again: a harsh, hollow wind. Air moving through a filter.

It was a breather; Qi'ra was sure of it. A White Worm was nearby, wearing an envirosuit.

Thankfully, Han heard it too. She felt him go perfectly still in the space beside her.

Moments later, a Grindalid slunk by, shoulders hunched, completely masked by the suit. Qi'ra didn't dare breathe.

Even after the Grindalid had passed, they waited a few moments before stepping back into the corridor and continuing on their way.

"That was close," Han whispered.

"If Lady Proxima has patrols out, that means she's already looking for us," Qi'ra pointed out.

"Then we go fast and quiet. We're almost there."

Han removed a grate from the wall while Qi'ra looked on, surprised. She hadn't realized that grate was removable.

They stepped inside the new tunnel—lower and darker than the rest—and Han replaced the grate behind them. After a couple of turns, a glow lit the corridor ahead. Han headed right for it, and they reached a crack in the wall.

Qi'ra peered inside and gasped. Someone lived here. It was a cave of sorts, with a fire pit in the center, a pallet along the wall that someone was using for a bed. A wind chime made of tiny rat skulls hung from the ceiling. Bones and food tins lay scattered everywhere.

"Han, what is this place?" she whispered.

"A friend of mine lives here," he said, slipping through the crack. "Looks like he's not home right now, but he won't mind us being here. I'm pretty sure."

"Pretty sure?"

"Almost totally sure."

She turned sideways and squeezed through. The place was warm, at least, and there was room to stand up straight. "So, we just lay low here for a while?"

"I guess." Han kicked some empty tins out of the way and sat on the floor.

"I don't think CorSec is going to give up looking for me."

He rested a hand on his pocket. "There's no way the Kaldana are going to stop looking for me."

Qi'ra cleared a space on the floor and sat beside him. By the light of the fire, she could clearly see how disgusting her shirt was. Her skirt was even more of a disaster. She didn't know anything about fabrics or laundering, but maybe there was a way to salvage the top. The skirt was a total loss; it would never show the deep, clean black of newness again, never mind the rip.

"How long do you think we can hide here?" she asked. She was already thinking about logistics. How would they get food? Maybe they could find a ratcatcher droid. They'd have to sleep in shifts. . . .

"Just long enough for you to make a plan," Han said.

"Oh, so *now* you want me to make a plan?"

He seemed confused. "Of course. You're good at that."

"Then why—"

"I was improvising, okay? Plans backfire. When that happens, I'm improvise guy." He was grinning at her, and Qi'ra couldn't decide if she wanted to grin back or punch his teeth out.

She looked away so she wouldn't do something she regretted, and said, "I met with a Kaldana rep today. You say they're after you?"

"Yeah. It was the weirdest thing." And without any hesitation at all, Han told her everything that had happened to him—the meeting in the bunker, the auction results, his friend Tool throwing a datacube to him while taking blaster fire, his flight through the sewers until he ran right into Qi'ra.

Qi'ra stared at him the whole time, and when he was

done, she realized that her mouth was slightly agape. More than anything, she wanted to see the datacube. What was in it that Lady Proxima was willing to spend a small fortune—before today, she would have considered it a *large* fortune—and risk their lives for? Qi'ra was finally putting the pieces together. "We were on the same mission," she said, her voice tinged with wonder. "Two different parts of it, but the same mission."

"I figured our assignments were related," he said.

Qi'ra hesitated to say more. Some tiny part of her hoped that the position of Head was still within her grasp. Maybe she should keep some information to herself. Maybe she shouldn't trust Han. He was likely to stab her in the back at the earliest opportunity, just like everyone else in her life.

Then she sighed. She had no choice. Teaming up with Han was her only chance at getting out of this alive. When he betrayed her . . . well, she'd deal with that when it happened.

"I was the one who presented the bid," Qi'ra said. "At the Buckell Center." She told him everything, leaving nothing out—how the White Worm bid had been dangerously, embarrassingly low; how angry the Kaldana woman had been when the Droid Gotra had won; how she'd barely escaped the room and the complex with her life.

Han studied her closely as she spoke, so closely that it made her feel funny. Exposed. Vulnerable.

When she was done, he rubbed his chin, considering. "That was quick thinking," he said, "learning the employee access code."

She shrugged it off, even though she was pleased at the compliment. "I have a good memory for stuff like that."

"So what do you think we should do now?"

"You still have that datacube?" Maybe he had hidden it somewhere. Or would say he had, just to keep it from her.

Han reached into a pocket and pulled it out.

Qi'ra stared at it. So much trouble for something so tiny. It was barely larger than the pad of her thumb.

"*This* is why the Kaldana Syndicate is after me now," Han said, brandishing it. "This tiny thing."

"Us," Qi'ra corrected. "They know I'm part of this."

"I knew the Kaldana Syndicate was a big deal," Han said. "But they're more powerful and better equipped than I realized."

Qi'ra nodded. "Their bid was six hundred and seventy-five million credits. So if they want us dead, they've got the resources to get the job done."

"And the Droid Gogo bid even more! A billion, you said."

"Gotra. Droid Gotra. And yeah. We White Worms weren't even in the running."

"Do you have an idea what the Gorpa is?"

The word *Gotra* died on her lips. How was Han even in competition with her for the job with Lady Proxima? She sighed. "Nope."

"Or any idea what's on this blasted cube?"

"Not the slightest idea."

Han said, "I think we have to find out."

"Maybe Lady Proxima—"

"No!" he interrupted. "Enough with this Lady Proxima mumbo jumbo. Just because you want a thing to be true doesn't mean it is. She doesn't care about you, Qi'ra. Like you said, that auction was an *embarrassment*. Now all of Corellia knows what a small-time player she is. She won't let something like that go. She'll have us both killed. Blame us publicly for everything to save face. She could even say that you messed up the bid and it was supposed to be much larger."

Qi'ra's face flushed warm because she hated being wrong. And yes, she kept going back to the idea of Lady Proxima helping them because she wanted it to be true. Was that so terrible?

"She made me a promise, you know," Han went on relentlessly. "Said if everything went well, she would name me Head. But now I realize she sent me on this assignment because I'm expendable. Just like anyone else."

Qi'ra felt as if the walls of the cave were closing in around her. "She promised you the promotion?" she said in a weak voice.

"Yep. No chance of that now, though."

"But she . . . she . . ."

"She promised it to you too?" he finished.

"How did you know?"

The right side of his mouth turned up into something that was not quite a smile.

"Let me guess," she said glumly. "A gut feeling."

"See what I mean? Lady Proxima doesn't care about us."

Qi'ra's stomach was in knots. She'd allowed herself to believe. To hope. Stupid, stupid girl. But she was smart enough to know sense when she heard it, so she said, "Fine. Not Lady Proxima. What do you suggest? How do we find out what's on that cube?"

Han poked a finger at the ground and started making circles in the dirt. "I dunno. We need someone with a datapad. Someone who can—"

"Tsuulo," she said. "He's our man. He got himself educated, remember? Before his family left Coruscant."

Han brightened. "You think he'd help?"

"Well, if we approach him, he'll either help or he'll go straight to Proxima. I guess it's a fifty-fifty chance."

Han frowned thoughtfully. "Sometimes it's better not to know the odds," he mumbled.

Qi'ra's urge to smack him began to fade. A little.

CHAPTER 6

Han had no idea how they were going to contact Tsuulo without getting caught. Every entrance to the den was sure to be guarded. In fact, Moloch had probably assigned double sentry shifts, and the tunnels surrounding the lair would be tightly patrolled. Tsuulo himself was likely in the bunk room getting some shut-eye. There was no way he or Qi'ra could sneak in and wake the Rodian.

They were still mulling it over in Old Man Powlo's cave when Qi'ra jumped up and dashed through the opening. Han was on his feet, ready to flee—he was certain she'd decided to go back to Proxima after all and rat him out—but she returned almost as quickly as she'd gone, and she was holding a whirring ratcatcher droid in her arms.

"Saw this fellow rolling by," she said, and suddenly she grinned the biggest, brightest, most amazing grin Han had ever seen in his life.

Had Qi'ra ever smiled before? He couldn't remember. And that smile was memorable. *I would have remembered that smile.*

"Uh . . . wow . . . That was . . . a good idea," he said.

"Well, maybe. It's not like we have anything to write with." She sat down, the droid cradled in her lap, and opened the trap compartment. "Hey, there's a dead rat inside," she said, reaching in for it.

"Don't throw it out," Han said. "We'll need it."

Qi'ra grimaced. "You're probably right."

"No, I mean for my friend. He likes gifts."

She froze for a split second, a suspicious look coming over her face, before pulling the limp rat out by its tail. "Okay, fine. A dead rat for your friend." Qi'ra tossed it to the ground near the fire pit. It was small, barely a meal, but it was something. "So how do we get a message to Tsuulo without having anything to write with?"

"You can read and write?" he said.

"Yes. You?"

He nodded. "I'm okay with Basic. A little Huttese. That's it though."

She said, "I guess I could use blood. Rip off a piece of this skirt and write on it."

He stared at her. Qi'ra was a strange, strange girl. "Um, no, not necessary. I have a dog biscuit."

"Like what Rebolt feeds his hounds?"

"Exactly." He pulled the remaining half biscuit from his pocket and was glad to discover it hadn't suffered too badly during his headlong flight through the sewer.

"Tsuulo gave this to me. So if we send it to him, he'll know it's from me."

Han rooted around near Powlo's sleeping pallet until he found a hard, sharp stick, and began to etch into the flat side of the biscuit.

Qi'ra moved to peer over his shoulder. She smelled awful, like laundry cleaner mixed with rotting vegetables. "What are you writing?" she asked.

"I think I'm saying 'help' in Huttese," Han told her. "That or 'urinate.' They're almost the same word."

"Well, at least no one else will be able to read it, if it's in Huttese."

"Exactly." Han thought for a moment, then scratched something else below it, in smaller, messier letters. "And this says 'more biscuits.' Well, I hope that's what it says." He put the biscuit back into the droid's trap compartment, then pressed the communicator button. "Find Tsuulo," Han said. "Bring him here."

He set the droid down. It gave one indignant bleep, then raced away, through the crack in the wall and hopefully straight to Tsuulo himself. The ratcatchers were barely self-aware, not like his friend Tool, who could evaluate and make decisions. *Sacrifice himself.* But Han was pretty sure the ratcatcher could find Tsuulo and bring him back.

"Now we wait," Han said.

Qi'ra settled herself cross-legged on the floor. She leaned her head back against the wall of the cavern. "You take first shift," she ordered.

"Why me?" he said, stifling a yawn.

"If I'm going to make the plans, I need to get some sleep so I can stay sharp." She closed her eyes.

Han frowned. He hated bossy people. But he took up a position near the opening that would allow him to keep watch.

He didn't realize he'd dozed until someone's hot breath against his ear woke him up. "Han. Friend," came the whisper.

Han startled but collected himself quickly. Powlo was staring at him, his golden gaze so close that Han realized the old fellow's irises really did glow. It wasn't just a trick of the light.

"Hi, Powlo," Han said. "I brought you a rat." He indicated the dead thing near the fire pit. "And another friend." He pointed to Qi'ra, who had slumped so oddly in her sleep that Han was sure she'd wake with a terrible crick in her neck.

"Mmmm, rat," Powlo said. "Mmmm, friend."

It was a bit disconcerting that those *Mmmms* sounded exactly the same.

Han moved toward Qi'ra, placing himself between her and Powlo, just in case Powlo was trying to say that friends were delicious.

This was the part Han hadn't thought through too well. He cleared his throat and told himself to be ready for anything. "So, Powlo, my friend. Is it all right if we stay here for a little while? We need a safe place."

Powlo cocked his head. "You visit?"

"Yes. Can we visit? For a few hours?"

Powlo shrugged. "Okay." With that, Powlo sat down beside the fire, grabbed the rat, and bit off its head.

"Well, that went well," Han muttered. Then he noticed that Qi'ra was awake and watching him.

"Did you call him Powlo?" she whispered. "You brought me to Old Man Powlo's territory?"

Yeah, maybe that had been a bad idea. But so far, so good, right? And when in doubt, brazen it out. "Sure did," he told her. "Powlo is a friend." Of course, Qi'ra didn't need to know that they'd just met, that he knew almost nothing about Powlo, that coming here had been a huge risk. "The White Worms will never think to look for us here."

Qi'ra straightened, rubbing at her neck. "They will, eventually. But you probably bought us some time." She eyed Powlo with distrust.

The strange creature eyed her right back, thoughtfully chewing his raw rodent. Then, mouth still full, he said to Qi'ra, "You ugly."

Han didn't know whether to laugh or come to Qi'ra's defense. He was pleasantly surprised to note Qi'ra's obvious amusement. "I'm . . . sorry about that?" she said, trying not to smile.

Powlo made a gesture toward her head. "Hair," he said. "Too much."

Qi'ra nodded solemnly. "I get that a lot."

A ruckus near the crack in the wall made both Han and Qi'ra shoot to their feet. The ratcatcher droid scooted in, followed by a small, green-skinned Rodian with mismatched antennae.

Powlo reacted instantly, sitting erect.

"No, Powlo. Friend," Han said. "This is another friend. Mmmm, friend."

"Tsuulo!" Qi'ra said.

"Hello, Han, Qi'ra."

"You came," Han said. He couldn't remember being so glad to see anyone in his life.

"Don't hug him just yet," Qi'ra said. "Tsuulo, did you tell anyone where you were going?"

Tsuulo blinked. "Of course not."

Qi'ra looked to Han, who translated for her.

"Swear it," she insisted. "Swear it on your dead parents."

"There is no need," Tsuulo said. "All is as the Force wills, and my word is my bond."

That made no sense to Han, but he translated anyway.

While Qi'ra tried to figure that one out, Powlo stepped forward and peered into Tsuulo's face. "Mmmm," he said.

Tsuulo started to back away. "Han? Who . . . what is this?"

"Mmmmm!" Powlo said. "Soooo beyootiful."

"I think he likes you," Han said.

Han introduced them, Powlo and Tsuulo both said the word *friend* a few times, and that seemed to be that. Powlo settled back down by the fire to finish his rat. Eyeing him warily, Tsuulo pulled a pack from his shoulder and reached inside.

"I brought dog biscuits," he said. "Proxima is looking for you both. She promised the position of Head to whoever finds you, so Rebolt is prepping his hounds now. He plans to sniff you out."

He handed each of them a dog biscuit while Han translated for Qi'ra. After a moment, Tsuulo tossed one to Powlo too, who rubbed it against his cheek.

"My money's on Moloch to find us," Qi'ra said. "Rebolt

isn't as competent, even with those hounds. Tsuulo, did you bring your datapad?"

"Always," Tsuulo said, retrieving it from his pack. "It took some doing to get here, by the way. Had to sneak past patrols. And you're welcome."

"Thanks," Han said. "I owe you one, pal."

"Yeah, you do. What do you need the datapad for?"

Han retrieved the cube and handed it over. "Everyone in the city of Coronet is looking for this. Maybe on all of Corellia. We need to know what's on it."

Tsuulo's eyes brightened. "Well, that sounds interesting." He inserted the cube into the datapad's port and fired it up.

A glow filled the cavern, bluish green and so much brighter than dying firelight. Holographic lines manifested, crisscrossing every which way. Some were accompanied by numbers, others by text. Tsuulo rotated his datapad so they could view it from every angle.

"What in all the galaxy is *that*?" Qi'ra said.

"Beeeyooootiful!" Powlo said.

"It's a blueprint," Tsuulo said.

"For what?" asked Han.

"Not sure. A shield, I think? No, a shield generator. It's . . ." Tsuulo swore, loudly and colorfully, using words Han had never heard before.

"What?" Qi'ra demanded. "What's wrong?"

"Han, what have you gotten me into?" Tsuulo asked. "These blueprints are Imperial property. They're stamped confidential, rated admiral and *above*."

"You're kidding me," Han said.

"Would someone please tell me what's going on?" Qi'ra demanded.

"These plans belong to the Empire," Han told her. "Lady Proxima, the Kaldana Syndicate, the Droid Gorpa . . . they were all bidding on secret Imperial tech."

Qi'ra opened her mouth. Closed it. And finally said, "Tsuulo, are you sure?"

He nodded. "I'm from Coruscant, remember?"

"Well, that explains the size of the bids," she murmured.

"I saw plans like this all the time in shop class," Tsuulo said. "Just, you know, *not* confidential. We made low-end motivators, power couplings, even small droids. But this . . . this is . . ." He peered closer, and the bluish lines reflected in his big black eyes.

"What? This is *what*?" Han said.

"This is complicated. Totally outside my experience. Part of it is still encrypted. A big part. The text refers over and over to someone called the Engineer. Does that mean anything to either of you?"

Han shook his head, then asked Qi'ra, who also shook her head.

Tsuulo glared at them both. "What's going on exactly?"

Powlo stared at Tsuulo and chewed his biscuit. "Mmmm."

Han didn't really trust Tsuulo, but that made him no worse than anyone else, and like it or not, the Rodian was part of it now. If Rebolt came looking with his hounds and found Tsuulo helping them, he'd be just as dead as Han and Qi'ra.

"I think we should tell him," Han said. "Everything."

Qi'ra said, "Now that he's helped us, he's in as much trouble as we are." She glanced over at Powlo, still crouched by the fire, admiring the blueprints floating in the air. "And I guess that means our *friend* will overhear, but I don't think there's any help for it."

So they told Tsuulo, leaving nothing out. His bug eyes got buggier and buggier until, finally, he slid to the ground and collapsed in a heap, muttering to himself.

"Tsuulo?" Han said, patting his shoulder. "You okay there, pal?"

"We have to give the cube back," Tsuulo said. "Before we all die."

"Yeah, great idea," Han said drily. "We should just

walk up to the Kaldana Syndicate, tap them on the shoulder, and hand it over."

Qi'ra said, "Maybe if we give it to Lady Proxima in exchange for our lives, she'll . . ."

She stopped herself. Han didn't even have to say anything.

"Sorry. Bad idea," she said.

"The Droid Gooper won the bid," Han pointed out. "We could give it to them, let them complete the transaction, wash our hands of it."

"No!" Tsuulo said. "The Droid Gotra are a bunch of terrorists."

Powlo seemed alarmed at Tsuulo's raised voice. Han kept an eye on the fellow as he translated the comment about terrorists.

"How do you know that?" Qi'ra asked. "How does he know that?"

"Everyone on Coruscant knows that," Tsuulo answered.

"What *is* the Droid Gorra?" Han asked.

Tsuulo's mouth opened, then closed. "I . . . don't actually know."

"He doesn't know."

"Anyway, giving it to them won't keep the Kaldana off our backs," Qi'ra said.

"What about the Engineer?" Tsuulo said. "The

mastermind behind the technology? If we gave it back to the original owner, maybe we'd get some gratitude. Some protection."

"You really want to tangle with Imperials?" Han asked.

"Might not be so bad," Tsuulo said. "The galaxy has been pretty peaceful since Palpatine became emperor. They're the good guys, right?"

"I'm not dealing with the Empire," Qi'ra said. "Having a high-end blaster and a fancy uniform doesn't keep someone from being a thug."

"Hey, you understood that?" Han said.

"Understood what?" she said. "I don't care what Tsuulo said, I'm not messing with Imperials. That's *always* a bad plan."

"Well, I think we should give it to the Kaldana, get them off our backs," Han said.

"I vote for the Empire," said Tsuulo.

"What if . . ." Qi'ra's voice trailed off, but her eyes were wide, her lips parted.

"What?" Han nudged.

Her voice was small, almost apologetic, when she said, "What if we sold it? We'd be rich. So rich." She held up the biscuit and stared at it. "We'd never have to eat rats or dog food again."

"And how would we arrange that?" Han said. "Don't get me wrong, I like money as much as the next guy, but we don't have the contacts, the influence."

"*You* might," she said. "You've been cultivating contacts all over the city; don't think I haven't noticed."

"And you've been planning something," he retorted. "Don't think *I* haven't noticed."

They glared at each other.

Tsuulo watched them both.

Powlo stared at Tsuulo.

"Trying to sell the cube would probably get us all killed," Tsuulo said finally. "We have no weapons, no experience. . . . We'd be the most hated beings in this sector."

Han translated, and Qi'ra sighed. "I think Tsuulo's right," she conceded. "Trying to sell the cube would be interpreted as a double cross by every single organization involved. Still . . ." She shrugged. "Better to do the double cross than be double-crossed, right?"

Han frowned. "It's also better to be poor and alive than rich and dead. Trying to sell it could get us killed."

They were silent for a long moment. The fire popped. Powlo stuck a finger in his mouth and began picking at his yellow teeth.

Han hated long silences. He said, "So, Miss I-Always-Have-a-Plan, what should we do?"

"Be quiet," she snapped. "I'm thinking."

Powlo stood and moved toward the crack in the wall. "More visitors!" he said.

Tsuulo swore. Han and Qi'ra both jumped to their feet.

"Now what?" Tsuulo whispered. Distant footsteps pounded through the sewer. They had moments before they would be discovered.

"We run," Qi'ra said.

CHAPTER 7

"But where?" Han said.

Qi'ra knew exactly where they should go, but it was hard to form the words. She'd kept the secret for so long.

"Qi'ra?" Han said. "You look like a hungry needle-gawp, opening and closing your mouth like that."

"I have a place," she blurted. "A safe house. I've been maintaining it for two years. It has supplies. A little bit of money. No one knows about it. If we can just get there, we'll be safe for a while."

"I was right!" Han said. "I knew you had a secret."

Tsuulo said something, but Qi'ra only caught the word for "distance." She could understand a few words of Huttese, but she wasn't about to let anyone know.

"He wants to know how far," Han said.

"It's . . . all the way across town. In the Bottoms."

Han's eyebrows went up. "Why would you keep a safe house there? That district is even worse than—"

"I have my reasons, all right?" Qi'ra's heart was racing, and only partly because the White Worm scrumrats were on the way. She hated revealing the safe house to anyone. It was so much a part of her.

"We can't get all the way to the Bottoms underground," Han said. "The sewers empty into a couple of those deepwater canals. It would put us right out in the open."

Tsuulo chirruped something.

"Yeah, of course it's faster to use the bridges, but who has money for a speeder cab?" Han responded. "Not me."

"We could steal money," Qi'ra said.

Tsuulo jumped to his feet, even as he removed the cube and powered down his datapad. The blueprint disappeared, leaving the cave feeling gloomy and cold. He stashed everything in his pack, chattering all the while.

"Tsuulo has an idea," Han said. "He knows where we can get access to a speeder. He says it's just outside the financial district, and we can be there before the sun goes down."

That was all Qi'ra needed to hear to get started. "Eat your dog biscuits now, because the route to the financial district will require us to swim. You both know how to swim, right?"

They nodded at her.

"We'll have to keep that datacube out of the water," Han pointed out.

Tsuulo said something angrily.

"*I* don't know how to keep it dry; hold it in your mouth or something. Rodians have dry mouths, right? Drier than humans', anyway?"

"We'll figure it out when we get there," Qi'ra said. "Now let's go!" She hated how necessity forced them to head out into danger without a solid plan. Her mind poked at possibilities, potential routes, contingencies as they packed up their few items and moved toward the crack and the low tunnel beyond.

"Friends, no," Powlo said.

Qi'ra paused and looked at Han, who simply seemed confused.

"What?" he asked.

"Friends. Stay."

"Look," Han said. "It's been great hanging out, and we really appreciate it, but we have to go before the White Worms find us."

Powlo scowled, and Qi'ra's heart started racing. Suddenly, he looked a lot less like Friend Powlo and more like the scary Old Man Powlo she'd been worried about all along. "Maybe he wants more food," she whispered urgently. "Do we have any more biscuits?"

Tsuulo fumbled with his bag and Han impatiently reached in to grab one. He leaned forward, offered it to

Powlo. "Here you go," he said. "Is this what you want?"

Powlo's eyes narrowed and his hand bolted out to grab the hard lump of fish-bread.

Qi'ra relaxed. . . .

The withered old creature screamed mournfully, flinging the biscuit at the wall, where it exploded in a shower of crumbs. "Friends! Stay!"

"Friends go!" shouted Han, shoving Qi'ra and Tsuulo through the crack.

He backed out after them, fending off Powlo's clutching hands while Powlo whimpered like an injured puppy.

"Which way do we go?" Qi'ra asked.

"That way!" Han said, pointing down a low tunnel, opposite the way they had entered. "Run!"

Qi'ra pushed Tsuulo ahead of her and started running. He babbled something she couldn't understand, but she pressed a hand into his back and willed him to run harder. Han caught up with her just as the tunnel twisted.

"Where are we going?" she shouted at him.

"I have no idea! I just know that Rebolt and his hounds are in the other direction!"

Powlo's wail of sadness chased them down the tunnel. If they hadn't been running for their lives, Qi'ra would have stopped and strangled Han that instant. He didn't have any kind of plan at all! Just a vague set of instincts that might be a gut reaction or might just be gas caused by eating dog biscuits.

"That way!" he shouted to Tsuulo, who turned down the side tunnel Han was pointing to. Qi'ra still had no idea where they were going, but the ceiling was a little higher, giving them more room to run.

Suddenly, the tunnel sloped downward. Tsuulo's feet slipped out from under him, and he splashed onto his backside and disappeared down a dark chute. Qi'ra stopped just in time at the very brink, and then Han bumped into her. They lost their footing in the slime, tumbled into the muck, and went careening down.

She braced herself for a hard impact into a grate or wall, but she shot out of the hole and dropped onto a giant bed of glowing fungus. Qi'ra rolled out of the way just in time to avoid Han landing on her.

Qi'ra scrambled to her feet, furious. "You idiot! You had no idea where we were going! You could have gotten us trapped! Or killed!"

Tsuulo said something she couldn't understand, but Han said, "I know!"

Han's admission took some of the fire out of her. Wait . . . *was* he admitting he'd been wrong? "You know *what*?" she asked suspiciously.

He stood up and paused to wipe some of the sticky

fungus off his elbows and out of his hair. Then he looked at her with a grin. "I know exactly where we are—and you do too."

She turned and really looked at the room. Knee-deep stagnant water, a variety of entrance shafts high on the wall, one main tunnel entering into the chamber, and a large circular drainage hole at the far end of the room. The sound of water trickling into the room and water dripping out—it was all very familiar.

Lady Proxima called it the Cistern of Discipline. Worms were sent here after storms to scavenge for flotsam. Sometimes they dropped nets down through the drainage hole to catch fleek eels and coppergrins.

More often, though, White Worms were sent here as punishment, for not meeting Lady Proxima's quotas or missing curfew too many times. The scrumrats would be tossed through the drainage hole into the giant underground basin below. If they could swim to the edge and find their way back, their transgressions were forgiven. Qi'ra had made it back, but not everyone did. The littlest ones struggled especially.

"This is the entrance to the Cistern of Discipline," she said.

"This is the entrance to the Cistern of Discipline," Han echoed enthusiastically.

"So if we go down the hole, we can swim to the

drainage tubes and make our way down toward the Bottoms."

"Right," Han said, jerking a thumb the other direction. "Or we can sneak back through the other tunnel toward the White Worm den, and—"

"Han," Tsuulo interrupted.

"Not now," Han said impatiently. "I'm trying to explain my plan."

Qi'ra heard, and then saw, the same thing Tsuulo did. She whispered urgently, "Han. Don't. Move."

"What?" he snapped, spinning around. "Just because . . ."

The words died on his lips. Standing at the entrance to the tunnel were three of Rebolt's hounds. Their large, bone-white bodies were machines of glistening muscle. The sharp wedges of their heads ended in ferocious jaws that could tear a man in half, framed by tentacle-like growths.

Where the hounds were, Rebolt would not be far behind.

The lead hound sniffed the air and growled. The other two spread out to flank Qi'ra, Tsuulo, and Han.

"Get behind me," Han whispered, putting himself between Qi'ra and the hounds.

"All the better for me to escape," she whispered, and

started edging back toward the drainage hole. Han followed her, step by step.

Tsuulo, on the other hand, walked right toward the hounds. He was going to sacrifice himself to give them a chance to escape—which was a terrible plan! He had the datacube, and they needed it if they were going to have any chance of survival.

"Don't do it, Tsuulo," she pleaded.

His one good antenna quirked in puzzlement, and then he reached into his bag—maybe he was going to throw her the cube!—and pulled out the rest of the dog biscuits.

The hounds closed on him like they were seeing an old friend. He gave one biscuit to each, and patted their sides while they rubbed their tentacled snouts against his face.

Rebolt's voice echoed down the tunnel, shouting for his hounds. The largest hound swiveled his head toward the voice, and then back toward Tsuulo, growling again.

"We need to go," she said, and she turned and ran for the drain.

There was nothing to do but jump.

She folded her arms tight to her chest, closed her eyes, and leaped.

The drop felt like it lasted forever, although it

couldn't have been more than nine or ten meters. She hit the water with a hard splash. Cold darkness closed in over her head. It was too easy to get disoriented in dark water, but she knew a trick. She calmed herself and allowed her body to sink until her boots met sludge. Then she kicked off the bottom and shot to the surface. As she treaded water and gasped for air, a second and third splash landed nearby.

Han's head popped up first, and he shook it like a wet dog, scattering water everywhere. Tsuulo popped up a moment later, and she could see the light glinting in his huge black eyes.

"The datacube," she said. "We can't let it get wet!"

Tsuulo opened his mouth and showed her the datacube on his tongue.

Han nodded enthusiastically. "Good thinking."

She was set to argue that a mouth wasn't much drier than a cistern, but the hounds stood at the edge of the drain above them and started howling. They had only seconds until Rebolt showed up, and if he didn't have a blaster, the White Worms who followed him would.

As one, they started swimming toward the far end of the reclamation basin and the overflow tubes. She dreaded the sound of a splash behind them, but no one followed, and moments later, they had climbed, breathless and dripping wet, onto a ledge at the end of the basin.

Rebolt's voice echoed through the massive underground chamber. "Come back. It will be worse for you if you don't."

Qi'ra was forming a suitably sharp response, but looking back at the water, she saw ripples from a school of fish—or something larger—cutting toward them. The White Worm scrumrats weren't the only ones who visited this cistern to find something to eat.

"Let's go," she cried, pushing Han and Tsuulo up the metal rungs of a ladder to the nearest overflow tube.

Seconds later, she clambered in behind them. It was pitch-black. "We can't walk down this tube blind," she said. "We could fall down a shaft, miss our turn. . . . Tsuulo, maybe you can use your datapad to light our way?"

Tsuulo mumbled something in reply, but she couldn't understand him.

"He says we have to wait for the datapad to dry out before turning it back on," Han translated.

"Can't he take the cube out of his mouth now?" She looked at her own soaked clothes and wet hands. "Never mind—there's no place drier to put it."

Tsuulo mumbled something again, but with the datacube in his mouth, even her basic Huttese failed her.

"No, I'm not trusting some old superstition!" Han said. "And Qi'ra isn't either."

Tsuulo blurted out a longer phrase, and Han calmed down.

"Oh, that works," he said. Then to Qi'ra, he explained: "He says not to worry—he can see really well in the dark."

"That's great," she said. "Why don't you lead the way, Tsuulo."

He said something else she couldn't understand. She waited for Han to translate, and then, after a moment, realized she was standing there alone. The only sound was her own breathing. They'd left without her.

I will not panic. I am not a panicker. With one hand on the wall, she began feeling her way down the black tunnel, hurrying until she stumbled right into someone.

"Han! Tsuulo!"

"We're right here," whispered Han. "Maybe you should hold on to my sleeve, and I'll hold on to Tsuulo's, so we don't get separated."

Tsuulo mumbled something.

Han said, "Yeah, I'm cold too. Stop complaining."

Qi'ra was beginning to shiver. Her stomach growled, and she regretted that Tsuulo had given the last of the biscuits to Rebolt's hounds. She'd been running and hiding all day, and was hungry and exhausted. But they couldn't stop yet. "Now let's *move*."

Hours later—feeling even hungrier and more exhausted—
Tsuulo led them up out of the tunnels and into a basement
beneath an old warehouse.

They reached a rusty arched gate that was their last
remaining barrier to escape. Light drifted down from a
gutter in the street above, but not much. Night was falling. They'd been running and hiding all day.

The gate was old, and it seemed to barely hang on its
hinges, but the latch was controlled by a modern access
pad. Qi'ra had never been here before; it was one of
the few areas Lady Proxima did not have entrée to. She
sized up the gate. Maybe with the right amount of force,
applied just so, they could pop it off its hinges.

She was just about to suggest as much when Han
stepped forward and pressed his thumb to the reader.
Something clicked. The gate swung open.

Qi'ra and Tsuulo stared at him.

"Hey, I get around, okay?" he said.

Tsuulo bleeped something. He had taken the datacube out of his mouth and was holding it in his fist. She
caught the word for "people."

"Yeah, I know some people here too," Han said. "If
you'd told me the speeder you had access to was at this
garage, I could have gotten us here quicker. I know a
shortcut."

Tsuulo chattered back angrily, something about "trust"

113

and "fodder," as the three of them stepped through the gate, closed it behind them, and found themselves confronted by a ladder. A rung was missing about two-thirds of the way up, but Qi'ra decided it looked sound enough.

Han climbed up first and disappeared through a hatch, then Tsuulo and, finally, Qi'ra. When her head crested the floor, her nose was assaulted by the scents of wet duracrete, overheated grease, and exhaust fumes. She climbed up onto the floor and sprung to her feet, ready for anything—blasters, CorSec, angry droids.

She needn't have worried. They were in an old warehouse, with high ceilings and pollution-fogged clerestory windows. Speeders were everywhere, every variety and color, in every possible state of repair. Beings and maintenance droids scurried all over the place, getting ready for something. A few attended the speeders themselves, checking gauges, tightening sockets, siphoning fuel from nearby tanks.

Two humans and one droid greeted Han; he'd obviously been here before. But no one else paid them any mind. Qi'ra felt her breathing ease.

All of a sudden, Tsuulo swore loudly. Qi'ra jumped before she realized that he was angry, not frightened. She was going to have to get him to teach her a few choice Huttese swear words. He obviously knew several.

He and Han talked back and forth a bit. Qi'ra gathered

that their arrival was terribly timed. A race was about to start, and the speeder Tsuulo had access to was no doubt lined up and ready to go.

"Which speeder?" Han asked. "I know a lot of people who rent space in this garage."

Tsuulo told him.

"You're kidding me!" Han said. "Reezo is your brother?"

Tsuulo made a sad sound.

"Yeah, don't get me started about family," Han said with a knowing sigh.

"It's your brother's speeder we're looking for?" Qi'ra asked.

Tsuulo nodded.

"Then why don't you just ask him to borrow it?" she suggested. "He wouldn't mind sitting out one race, right?"

Tsuulo protested vehemently.

"He and his brother don't talk," Han said. "Or maybe Tsuulo doesn't talk to Reezo? They haven't said a word to each other in six months. Anyway, he says there's absolutely no way Reezo would skip a race. Racing is everything to him."

Qi'ra didn't know much about racing, only that there was the legal kind and the illegal kind, and the kind that happened in this part of the city, with these color-drenched, souped-up speeders, was definitely the illegal kind. It was such a part of the local culture, though, that CorSec mostly looked the other way. Sometimes a fatal accident would occur, or property owned by an important citizen would get damaged, and CorSec would make a show of busting someone and decrying the practice of illegal street racing. But after a little time had passed and the good people of Coronet had forgotten to be shocked and angry, everything would go back to normal.

"Maybe someone else has a speeder we could borrow?" Qi'ra suggested.

Han and Tsuulo gaped at her.

"What? What did I say wrong?"

"You don't just ask to borrow someone's speeder," Han said.

Tsuulo nodded vigorously.

"It's like asking to borrow someone's spouse. Or their soul."

"That makes no sense."

Han looked down at the ground. "It does to some of us."

"You have a better idea?"

"Well, no . . ." A maintenance droid flew by, startling them all, but it paid them no mind. "I mean yes!" Han said. He looked up at her, his face shining with that abominable grin.

"Uh-oh," said Qi'ra.

Han grabbed Qi'ra and Tsuulo by the shoulders and brought them close so the three of them were head to head. He whispered, "We grab Reezo. Tie him up. Take his place in the race."

Qi'ra blinked. "That might be the worst idea I've ever—"

"Hear me out. The race route takes us right down Narro Sienar Boulevard, across all the downtown bridges. When we're near the Bottoms, we'll veer off track. No one will question what happened. They'll just assume we blew a valve or something."

A few speeders rumbled past, cruising out toward the street. One belched dirty gray smoke. Another whined, high-pitched and metallic like a rusty nail scraping a mirror. The race was starting soon. Whatever they decided, they had to do it quickly.

"All right, maybe that's not the *worst* plan," Qi'ra admitted. "Tsuulo, what do you think?"

Tsuulo jabbered something while bobbing his head up and down.

Han gave him a weird look, but he translated: "He *loves* the idea of tying up his brother. Apparently, they *really* don't get along."

"Then let's do it," Qi'ra said. "Tsuulo, lead the way."

Tsuulo set off toward the far corner of the garage, and the others followed.

"How are we going to do this?" Han whispered.

"Reezo hasn't seen his brother in a long time, right?" Qi'ra said. "I figure he'll be really surprised. While he's distracted, you sneak up behind him."

"And do what?"

"I don't know, hit him over the head with a wrench or something."

"Qi'ra, I don't want to hurt anyone."

"Better him than us."

Tsuulo froze in his tracks. He turned and whispered something.

"That's Reezo," Han said, pointing.

Another young Rodian crouched beside a speeder. His skin had a slightly yellower cast than Tsuulo's and he seemed a couple of years older. A pair of massive goggles hung from his neck, sized for Rodian eyes.

But it was the speeder Reezo was tinkering with that took Qi'ra by surprise. It was huge and unwieldy, as green and shiny as an emerald, and it hovered closer to the ground than all the other speeders. Qi'ra couldn't tell if the repulsorlift was broken or if it was meant to be that way. Florescent green light rimmed the lower edge, making the oil-slicked cement beneath glow like a rotting swamp. Two stems, each ending in a disk, protruded from the hood; it took Qi'ra a moment to realize the twin receivers were colored and contoured to look like Rodian antennae.

"Holy moons, that thing looks like a giant green bug," Qi'ra whispered.

"I was thinking hover-brick," said Han. "It gets worse, though."

"What do you mean?"

Reezo was oblivious to their presence. He leaned over the seat and hit a switch on the console. Holographic flames shot out from the fender and rear spoiler, dancing bluish and hazy in the air. Qi'ra imagined that while the speeder was racing, the flames would appear to stream behind.

"That's what I mean," Han said. "Also, he removed the dampener from the engine coil so it would be as loud as possible."

Sure enough, Reezo fired it up, and the whole warehouse rumbled so loudly Qi'ra felt it deep in her chest.

She stretched on her tiptoes and leaned toward Han's ear so he could hear over the noise. "We should make our move now! That horrible sound will cover any scuffle."

Han nodded, but then he paused. "Are we *sure* we want to do this?" he asked them both.

Tsuulo twittered something in Huttese that even Qi'ra could tell was an enthusiastic affirmative.

"No, I don't have a better idea," Han said glumly.

With Tsuulo leading the way, the three of them crept forward.

CHAPTER 8

Han had been in his share of scuffles, sure. Like the time that Grindalid caught him cheating at sabacc. Well, not *cheating* exactly. He was still figuring out how the game was played and had made an honest mistake.

Then, like always, Han had faced him down. He either came away from a fight victorious or crawled away bloody, but he didn't back down. In fact, he preferred direct confrontation to innuendo, sneaking around, or the complicated planning Qi'ra seemed to prefer.

But that didn't mean he went looking for trouble. And it didn't mean he particularly liked hurting people. So as Tsuulo walked up to his brother and tapped him on the shoulder, Han's gut was in a knot.

Reezo spun around, and his long snout-mouth dropped open. "Tsuulo?" he squeaked out. "What are you doing here?"

Han grabbed a pilex driver that was lying on a tool cart and began to circle around behind Reezo.

"Reezo," Tsuulo said, his voice full of barely contained

rage. "I see you've spent even more of our inheritance. Holo-flames? Really? I thought you said the money had run out."

"I won some," he said, wiping his hands on his pants. "By racing. I'm getting a lot better."

Tsuulo snorted. Han raised the pilex driver and prepared to whack Reezo over the head. Then he got a better idea.

A long rag swung from Reezo's back pocket. Han whipped it out, flipped it over Reezo's head and into his mouth, and yanked him backward. Reezo started to flail, reaching for the gag, but Han kicked the back of his knee. Reezo crumbled to the ground, dragging Han with him.

"Someone grab his arms, quick," Han said. "There's some cable on the tool cart—"

A small form darted forward. Before Han could blink, a fist crashed into Reezo's face. The Rodian boy swayed a moment, then slumped over, unconscious.

Han looked up to find Qi'ra standing over them, cradling her right fist. "Ouch," she said. "That hurt."

"I'm sure Reezo sympathizes," he said drily. "Here, help me get him out of sight."

Tsuulo ran forward. "Is he okay?"

"I think so," Han said, dragging Reezo's limp form

behind the speeder. "Just knocked out is all. You hit people often?" he asked Qi'ra.

"I've been wanting to hit someone all day," she said.

"Anyone in particular?"

She glared at him.

"Forget I asked."

That was some hook. Han had been on the streets a long time, and he could count on one hand the number of times he'd seen someone get knocked out with a single hit from a human. Maybe Qi'ra had an aptitude for fighting. She seemed to have an aptitude for a lot of things.

"We can't leave him in the middle of the garage," Qi'ra said, looking around to see if they'd been noticed. The garage was nearly empty now, with all the speeders outside getting ready to race. "We have to stash him somewhere."

"There's a tool closet over there," Tsuulo suggested.

"Everyone uses that closet," Han said. He looked back and forth between Tsuulo and Qi'ra. He knew exactly where they should stash Reezo, but saying as much would reveal his most closely guarded secret.

Or maybe not. Maybe he could manage to only *sort of* reveal it.

"Over there," Han said, indicating a direction with his head. "That gray speeder. Hurry."

Qi'ra and Tsuulo each grabbed a leg. Reezo swinging between them, they moved toward the very heart of everything Han had been working toward for the past two years.

"Huh," said Qi'ra as they approached. "I don't know much about speeders, but isn't this one missing its . . . engine?"

"Yeah," he said, already regretting this. "That's why we can stash Reezo here. The whole engine compartment is empty."

"And check out that windshield!" she went on relentlessly. "It looks like it was salvaged from an old Flash speeder. Holy moons, what a piece of junk."

"It's not junk!" he snapped before he could think better of it.

Her eyebrows went up, and then she burst out laughing. "This is *your* speeder! This is why you're almost always late getting back to the lair."

Han opened the access hood. "I think you mean 'always almost late,' " he grumbled. Tsuulo and Qi'ra helped him lift and shove Reezo until the older Rodian fell into the empty compartment, all in a heap. Han slammed the compartment closed. "This speeder doesn't look like much," he felt compelled to explain, "but I don't care about that. It's going to be the fastest speeder the Corellian streets have ever seen. I'm building the repulsorlift from scratch, see. Then I'm going to add stabilizers for extra maneuverability, maybe paint it blue."

Qi'ra shrugged. "If you say so—"

"What are you doing?" came a distinctly feminine voice. The three whirled.

"Beejay," Han said, putting his hands up. "I can explain."

A mechanical repair droid stood before them, hands fisted at her waist. She had a single round eye in the middle of her gunmetal-gray head and a grill for a mouth. A brown tool belt was slung over one shoulder.

"You know each other?" Qi'ra asked, but her eyes were darting everywhere, evaluating. That girl never stopped thinking.

"Beejay-Sixty-Four's a friend," Han assured her. "She's been helping me figure some things out. You trust me, don't you, Bee? You know I wouldn't do anything wrong."

BJ-64 whipped a hex wrench from her tool belt and brandished it, advancing on Han.

"Without a good reason," he amended hastily. "You know I wouldn't do anything wrong without a good reason."

"Reezo rents space in this garage just like you," BJ-64 said. "That means he's guaranteed safety, for him and his speeder. I saw what you did. I'm afraid I have to comm the garage owner."

A horn sounded somewhere outside, followed by cheering. "The first race is off," Tsuulo said. "We can still make the second if we hurry."

BJ-64 said, "No racing for any of you tonight."

"Look," Han said. "We're not going to hurt Reezo. I mean, any more than we already did. We just need to use his speeder for a while."

"That thing?" she exclaimed. "That *abomination*? The only good use for Reezo's speeder is molten scrap." She continued to advance, hex wrench held high.

"I'll make a deal with you, Bee. You let us go, don't comm anyone, and I'll strip Reezo's speeder."

The hex wrench faltered in the air. "Oh?"

"We'll remove the holo-flames attachment, strip the extra fuel pump and the bounce package—"

"The under-lighting too?" she said. "The battery compartment creates a drag, you know, and when he puts it on the flash setting, it causes a hitch in the idle."

She was listening. This was going to work. "Absolutely. The under-lighting goes too."

"I guess the antennae should stay. They're part of his 'cultural heritage' as he puts it."

"Sure, Bee, whatever you say."

She lowered the hex wrench. "Fine. Take that thing

out of my garage. Can I free Reezo from your engine compartment after the races?"

"We'd appreciate it if you did."

"How are you going to pilot it?" she asked. "His controls are encrypted."

"Leave that to me," said Tsuulo. "Come on, we have to hurry."

Han waved jauntily to his friend. "Thanks, Bee! See you soon!" He hoped. If he didn't get himself killed tonight.

"What was that about?" Qi'ra asked as they ran for the emerald green hover-brick. "How did you know what to say to that droid?"

"I'll explain later." They reached Reezo's speeder, which was still idling loudly, ready to go. "You sure you can do this, Tsuulo?"

"Completely sure!" Tsuulo closed his eyes, breathed through his snout for a moment, and then said calmly, "The Force will be with me."

"Whatever you say, pal." Tsuulo wasn't the only religious person Han had known. And it seemed that the poorer people got on Corellia, the more its centers for religious worship overflowed. He'd heard that the Temple of the True Vine now offered three services per day to accommodate. Han didn't buy any of it, not one word. He didn't believe in any god—not a Maker or a

Force, neither a sun nor a moon. But if someone took comfort and inspiration from religion, who was he to argue? As long as they didn't argue with him.

The speeder dashboard was a jumble of gauges and wires; Han had no idea how Tsuulo was going to figure it out. But after composing himself, the Rodian reached right in. He plucked a wire here, reattached it there, changed a setting, then plugged his datapad into a port and keyed in a few things with his long suction-cup fingers.

The speeder lowered itself to the ground for easy access, and the door slid open.

Han couldn't believe it. "How did you do that?"

Tsuulo shrugged. "I never ask how I'm going to do something. I just believe I can do it."

"Huh." Han started to climb in.

"Into the back seat," Qi'ra ordered. "I'm piloting."

Han wanted to drive this speeder so badly it was like a pain in his chest. "You know how to pilot a speeder?" he asked.

"I had to learn for one of Lady Proxima's assignments. I've had a few lessons."

Well, Han could drive a little too, but he'd never had *lessons*. Reluctantly, he climbed into the back seat. Tsuulo followed, they slid the door shut, and Qi'ra gently guided the speeder from the garage bay and into the Corellian night.

"I can't believe we're doing this," Qi'ra said. "I can't believe this is working."

"It's not working yet," Han pointed out. Rumbling speeders were lined up two wide and several deep. The only race position remaining was the back left. It was the absolute worst position to pull in a street race. Luckily, they didn't have to win. They just needed to make a good show of it while getting across town.

The speeder lurched forward as Qi'ra guided it into position. "Sorry about that!" she called. "This accelerator is touchy."

"You sure you know what you're doing?" he called back. The pale blue holographic flames shimmied and danced around them.

"Just punch the accelerator when it's time to go and don't crash, right?"

Han had a bad feeling.

"It's good we ended up in the rear position," Qi'ra said over her shoulder. "There's no one behind to keep an eye on us, see our amateur driving. And we can just drift away once we're across town."

She had barely finished her sentence when another speeder pulled in right behind them. "Blast," Qi'ra said as Tsuulo swore, using a string of words that Han was pretty sure described a Gamorrean in an anatomically improbable position.

The speeder behind them was deepest black, and it rumbled heavily. Han couldn't see the pilot; the speeder's headlamps were too bright, and they fluttered, giving him a slight headache. Han figured it was a purposeful modification, meant to confuse other racers. "Don't look at the light," Han warned Qi'ra. "It's meant to throw you off."

He saw her hands tighten on the controls.

"You can do this," he added. Qi'ra was good at everything, he told himself. And she'd had lessons. She'd be fine.

The street ahead was dark, dangerously so. When it came to illegal street racing, no one bothered to light the routes or follow standard safety protocols. The speeders themselves lit the street, and a soft glow came from either side as onlookers keyed in to datapads, making last-second bets. A nimbus of light far ahead marked central Coronet and its resident nightlife. The race would take them right past it, into the darker, more dangerous part of the city.

A Pa'lowick woman strode between the speeders toward the front, sashaying as she went. She held aloft a large white flag in her skinny arms, grimed with dirt and rust. The fabric rippled in the night breeze.

The crowd went silent. It seemed that the thunder of idling speeders was the only sound in the world. It surrounded Han, filled him up, buoyed him. He found himself clutching his right hand, as if he could prep the accelerator by the force of his will.

The Pa'lowick woman waved the flag. Around and around it went until, suddenly, she swished it down and out of sight. The speeders ahead of them burst forward.

Qi'ra hit the accelerator, and their green brick lurched forward, swung crazily to the left, and almost tipped over.

"Qi'ra!" Han yelled.

"Sorry!" she yelled back. But she got the speeder righted and zoomed to catch up with the others. Holo-flames streamed behind them, making the speeder seem as if it were on fire.

Wind slicked Han's hair back, and his eyes stung, streaming with tears. He should have thought to snag racing goggles for all of them. No matter; this was going to work. Qi'ra was doing just fine.

They approached their first turn. They were several lengths behind the pack, except for the black speeder with flickering lights, which seemed content to draft on them for a while. No worries. In fact, it was better to not be in a hurry. Still, Han couldn't help yearning for a little more speed, a little more excitement. He wanted to see those others speeders up close and in action, listen to their purring repulsorlift engines, breathe deep of their exhaust. Was there any better smell than speeder exhaust? He couldn't think of one.

His breath hitched when he realized something important: Qi'ra was not braking or banking for the turn.

Tsuulo started hollering that she was going too fast.

"Yes!" Qi'ra yelled. "I heard these racers take turns hard! Best way to corner efficiently!"

Experienced racers, sure. Not someone who'd only piloted a speeder a handful of times.

Qi'ra slammed into the turn. The rear end of the speeder skittered out from under them, careening into the base of a streetlamp. Han's neck jerked with the impact, and he grabbed at the roll bar, expecting to flip. Qi'ra hit the accelerator, powering them out of a potential crash, but Han could hear the whine of compromised metal. He looked behind them just in time to see the streetlamp crash to the ground, showering sparks.

The black speeder was still behind them, but it was choosing to remain at a safe distance. Smart.

"I think we almost died back there," Han called out.

"This is harder than it looks!" Qi'ra admitted.

Tsuulo started muttering.

"What was that?" Han asked.

"I'm praying to the Force," Tsuulo said.

Han didn't know much about religion, but he was

pretty sure the Force wasn't something one prayed to. Now was not the time to argue, because they were approaching another turn.

He caught a whiff of exhaust, and taillights flashed ahead. Qi'ra had managed to gain on the others.

"This is a much tighter turn!" Tsuulo yelled.

"What?" Qi'ra yelled back.

"It's a switchback," Han explained. "The turn doubles back on itself, so you'll have to be ready."

"Should I go faster?" she said.

"No!" he and Tsuulo said in unison.

"Are you sure we should turn?" she said. "That's the wrong direction for us."

"You're overthinking," Han said. "The race route will get us there; just trust the road, and trust the speeder."

"That makes no sense! Hold on, I'm going to speed up, then swing around the corner, pivot us on the speeder's fulcrum."

"No!" they both said again.

"Han, help," pleaded Tsuulo, then, to himself: "Force be with us, Force be with us, Force be with us."

The air lit up around them, flickering like a nightmare. The black speeder was making its move.

"I can't see!" Qi'ra cried.

Though light-blind, Han thought he could detect a shape ahead and to the left. A regular landspeeder.

Someone hadn't gotten the message that this road was supposed to remain vacant for the night. It was parked between them and their switchback turn, and Qi'ra was aiming right for it.

Tsuulo swore.

Han jumped over the seat into the front. "Get in the back," he ordered, grabbing for the controls.

"I can do it! I've been doing—"

"Now!" he barked.

Clinging for her life to the roll bar, Qi'ra clambered over the seat into the back while Han slid into the spot she'd just vacated. He spent a precious moment orienting himself to the controls—accelerator, right reverse thruster, left reverse thruster, power gauge, and . . . a hover adjustment lever? Oh, right; this abomination had a bounce package.

The black speeder pulled up beside them, and the pilot shouted obscenities. Tsuulo made a rude gesture right back.

It sped past, much to Han's relief, and he prepared to take them into the turn. Easy on the accelerator, gentle tap on the left reverse thruster followed by harder tap right to pivot just so . . . The regular landspeeder came into view; it was *way* closer than he'd realized.

"Han, look out!" Qi'ra called.

Han punched the hover adjustment lever. A *whoosh*

took his breath away as Han's rear pressed into the seat and their racing speeder jetted upward about four meters. It soared over the parked speeder. Han let out a yell of triumph.

Then his heart leaped into his throat as they crashed back down. The speeder's belly skimmed the road, leaving a trail of sparks, before the repulsorlift kicked back in and their ride smoothed out.

Han steered into the turn with ease. The road became a bridge as they crossed over one of Coronet's many waterways.

"Well, that takes care of the under-lighting," Tsuulo yelled over the sounds of engine and wind. "Pretty sure we left it back at that intersection."

"Think you can catch up to the others?" Qi'ra said. "We should at least make it *look* like we're trying."

They faced another hairpin turn, and Han took it gently. Before them stretched a vast straightaway that would take them exactly where they wanted to go. In the distance, the taillights from the other racing speeders glowed like beacons against the night. Han grinned and hit the accelerator.

He doubted Reezo's speeder was up to the task of catching up. The Rodian seemed more interested in useless accoutrements than speed and power. It wasn't a philosophy Han shared.

So he was pleasantly surprised to notice the lights ahead getting gradually closer and closer. Maybe the Rodian knew a little something about custom building after all.

Water continued to stream from his eyes, and wind plastered his hair back. His damp clothes were icy against his skin, and he could hardly feel his fingers. This far back, away from the pack, they had the empty street all to themselves. He swept side to side, just to get a feel for the controls, and the speeder responded with gratifying agility. It was like skimming air. No, like flying.

The roots of Han's teeth began to ache; he realized he hadn't stopped grinning into the cold wind since he'd taken over the pilot's seat.

Qi'ra tapped him on the shoulder. "We're getting close," she said in his ear. "I recognize this part of town."

He gave the accelerator another light boost—too much fuel would clog the lines, slow them down—and he was delighted when the speeder shot forward. Along the road, steam rose from sewer vents as the night temperature continued to drop. They crossed another bridge, and streetlamps cast shards of rusty orange onto the lapping black water. Ahead of them, the other racing speeders banked right; the route would loop around central Coronet, then back to Narro Sienar Boulevard and the garage.

"Keep going straight," Qi'ra ordered.

They left the boulevard and dipped downward, away from the city lights, into the district known as the Bottoms.

Rebolt had once told them that the Bottoms used to be an old swamp, before shipbuilders had drained the land to put up more factories. No sewers led here; the land was too low, the water table too high. After decades of industry, pollution and water seepage had rendered the area all but unusable. It was a land of storage lots and junkyards, and sometimes it was hard to tell the difference between them. Only the poorest and most desperate lived and worked in the Bottoms. Han found it strange that Qi'ra would keep a safe house here.

The street narrowed, and Han was forced to slow down. Decay surrounded them—boxy warehouses with broken windows, ramshackle huts made of scrap metal, and ragged beggars huddling beneath makeshift eaves. The air smelled of wet soot and burned meat.

Though it was nighttime, everyone was about their business. Music drifted toward them, coming from the glowing open windows of a cantina. They passed a line of beings waiting at a rickety food stand that advertised eel skewers. Han's stomach growled. As soon as they were settled in Qi'ra's safe house, he'd eat that dog biscuit he'd saved against her advice. Unless it was soaked in sewage from his swim. Well, actually, maybe even then.

Qi'ra leaned forward and said, "Turn left at the intersection."

It was hardly an intersection, more like the confluence of a few crooked alleys, but he did as directed.

"We'll have to hide the speeder," she said. "Any working vehicle in this district gets stripped clean before you can blink."

"Where should we hide it?" Han asked.

"Just go where I tell you."

She sounded cold and brusque, even more than usual. Maybe she was sore about him taking over the pilot's seat.

Qi'ra directed them through the warren of alleys and crooked side streets with confidence. The land sloped lower and lower. The cracked duracrete began to sheen with wetness. Here and there, stubborn weeds grew in clumps, clinging to any patch of soil they could find—in the cracked streets, along the walkways, even on rooftops.

The buildings parted, revealing utter darkness. Han adjusted the light setting so he could see his way forward.

A vast, swampy field stretched ahead, filled with long, stubborn grass and pollution-stunted trees. Giant, building-sized lumps dotted the field, like massive toads ready to spring. As they approached, the lumps manifested into something more recognizable, and Han gasped.

They were starships. Hundreds of them. All abandoned hulks, stripped of anything useful, rotting in the swamp.

"The freighter boneyard," Tsuulo whispered reverently. "I've heard of it, but I've never been here before."

"Circle around the western edge," Qi'ra said, pointing.

They cruised by a looming shell of metal that in the distant past had housed a high cockpit centered above twin propulsion jets. A clothesline hung between the massive jets, and grimy fabric fluttered in the breeze.

"People live here," Han breathed.

"People live everywhere," Qi'ra said. "Always. No matter what. They find a way."

"Is one of these ships your safe house?" he asked.

Qi'ra said nothing.

"We'll have to be careful," Tsuulo said. "This is Silo territory."

Everyone had heard of the Silo, a work camp filled with orphans, run by the nastiest people Corellia had ever seen, where the life expectancy was less than eighteen cycles. Word on the street was the Silo made the White Worm den seem like a palace of luxury and decadence.

"There!" Qi'ra said. "See that big tree? Pull the speeder in behind it."

Trees were uncommon in and around Coronet, so this one was easy to spot even in the dark—a stunted thing with a huge trunk that grew from the side of a hill, reaching desperately for sunshine it hardly ever found. Behind the tree was a depression of sorts, an indentation in the land that made for a perfect hidden parking spot.

Han turned off the speeder and jumped out. His boots made a squelching sound as he landed; they were smack-dab in the middle of a bog.

Qi'ra and Tsuulo landed beside him. Now that the speeder was turned off, they were in almost total darkness. A hint of moonlight diffused through thick clouds, giving both Tsuulo and Qi'ra a bluish cast to their skin.

"So . . ." Han said, looking around at a big black nothing. "This is it?"

Solemnly, with obvious reluctance, Qi'ra said, "Welcome to my . . . home, I guess."

She turned, bent toward the steep hill, and yanked at something. An entire layer of sod lifted away, revealing a doorway.

CHAPTER 9

Qi'ra's hands shook as she pulled up the sod that camouflaged the entrance to her safe house. She had spent years fixing this place up. She'd poured sweat and tears and all the credits she could scavenge into it. And by showing it to Han and Tsuulo, she was giving it up.

Bringing them here was a necessity, she told herself. Now that the Kaldana, the White Worms, the Droid Gotra, and maybe even the Empire were all after them, the only safe place was the one no one knew about.

But now Han and Tsuulo knew, and after tonight, things would never be the same.

Qi'ra shoved aside the fuselage scrap that served as her doorway and beckoned them into the dark. She felt their presence at her back as she groped along a shelf for the lamp . . . there! She fumbled for the switch. Light flooded the room, searing her eyes.

Han and Tsuulo stood gaping.

"It's a ship!" Han said.

"Well, we *are* in the freighter boneyard," she pointed out.

"Yeah, but from outside, it looked like . . ."

Qi'ra shoved the fuselage scrap back into place, sealing them in against the night. "I found this place a while back," she explained. "Half buried. There was hardly room to stand up, but the structure seemed sound." She reached up and caressed an arched gray beam. Several of them all in a row gave the room shape, like the metal ribs of a giant beast. "I excavated it and took the dirt outside, covered over the rest. Now only the people who live here in the boneyard know that my hill is actually a ship."

Tsuulo asked her something, and she looked to Han.

"He wants to know if you have power. If not, he says he can rig something for you."

A funny feeling twinged in her chest. It was the feeling she always got when someone wanted to do something nice for her and she didn't know if there were strings attached.

"Thanks, but no," Qi'ra said. "I thought about setting up some solar panels, but they'd just get stolen. I have a few items here that run on fuel, but fuel is really expensive. . . ." Suddenly, she saw the place through their eyes: cold, dark, with only a crooked shelf, a sagging cot, and a rusty table and chairs for furnishings. The ceiling was too low for them to stand up straight. Not to mention the constantly seeping floor. She never set her belongings on the ground. They'd be ruined in less than a day.

She sighed. The thing she took the most pride in in all the galaxy was a rotting garbage heap. "Sorry," she said glumly. "I know it's not much, but at least we'll be safe—"

"It's amazing," Han said. "It's perfect."

Tsuulo nodded enthusiastically.

Qi'ra's face warmed. She wasn't sure why their opinion mattered, but somehow it did. "Well, make yourselves at home. Let's get some sleep. Then we'll make a plan. We should sleep in shifts. The table is durable enough for sleeping. And the cot. One person can keep watch out in the speeder."

Han and Tsuulo exchanged glances, then they both plopped down into chairs. Tsuulo leaned his forearms on the table and slumped over, as if relieved to find something sturdy.

"So . . . no sleeping?" Qi'ra said.

"I feel like I'm going at hyperspeed," Han said. "Might be a while before I can fall asleep."

Qi'ra knew exactly what he was talking about. Though her body was exhausted, her mind was too busy for sleep.

Tsuulo said something about Reezo.

"He hopes his brother is suffering and scared right

now," Han said, pulling the dog biscuit out of his pocket. It crumbled to pieces in his hand, and he stared down in disgust.

"I wouldn't eat that," Qi'ra said, remembering their swim through sewage.

"Might not have a choice," Han said, but he brushed all the pieces onto the table instead of putting them into his mouth.

"Tsuulo," Qi'ra said. "Why do you hate your brother so much?"

The Rodian bleeped in protest.

"He doesn't *hate* him exactly," Han explained. "They just don't get along." After a pause, Han added, "So are you going to tell us or not?"

The line of tiny spines along Tsuulo's scalp fluttered, and his mouth turned down. Then he started talking. With Han's help, Qi'ra gathered the gist of it.

Tsuulo and his brother, Reezo, were born on Coruscant. They went to school there. Tsuulo loved school so much he took extra classes via the local holonet. He didn't have a knack for languages or literature; like many Rodians, he struggled to speak Basic. But he was a natural in his engineering courses. He wanted to design hyperdrives someday.

Their mother was a sales rep for a small freighter company, and her work often took her offworld. One year, after winning a big sales bonus, she decided to take the whole family with her on one of her business trips. "It will be a great education for the boys," she'd said to her husband. So off they went, all four of them, to Corellia for a sales conference at the famous Buckell Center.

On the second morning of the conference, while Tsuulo and his brother were sleeping in, their parents left for an early breakfast. They were strolling toward a nearby restaurant when a speeder cab swerved off the thoroughfare and missiled into them, killing them instantly before crashing into Diadem Square.

It turned out the speeder cab had been hijacked by an angry factory worker, a young Besalisk male who recently had lost his job. He'd been aiming the speeder for the employment office. Tsuulo's parents had just been in the way.

Tsuulo paused at this point and blinked a few times.

"You don't have to tell us any more if you don't want to," Qi'ra said. She knew what it was like to have secrets. Giving them to others felt like peeling parts of yourself away. Even the seemingly unimportant secrets.

Because when you had nothing, your secrets were everything.

But maybe a little sympathy was all Tsuulo needed, because he started talking again, even faster than before.

Later that day, when CorSec found the boys and

told them what had happened to their parents, Reezo assured them he was old enough to take care of his little brother, that there was no need to send them to an orphanage or a work camp. A few days later, an insurance settlement came through from Coruscant. If Tsuulo and Reezo were very careful, the money their parents had left them would pay for their educations and get them on their feet.

But Reezo had a better idea. He'd heard about Corellian speeder racing and become obsessed with the idea. Without consulting Tsuulo, he used the insurance settlement to purchase a speeder and enter his first race. He was sure he could double their money with his winnings.

He crashed the speeder, leaving them broke.

When Tsuulo found out, he was furious. Reezo seemed to feel awful about it, but no matter how many credits came their way—through begging, through odd jobs, through selling all the clothing and items their parents had brought with them from Coruscant—Reezo couldn't keep himself from spending it on his new hobby. Finally, six months before, Tsuulo had left his brother behind, certain he'd be better off on his own. He left with nothing but the clothes on his back and his datapad.

He'd been so relieved to get accepted into the White

Worm gang. Then he ate at least once per day—a big improvement over being with Reezo.

So no, he didn't hate his brother. His brother was trying, in his own way, to make things right. But Tsuulo still hoped he was suffering, alone and scared in the engine compartment of Han's speeder. Reezo had it coming.

After Tsuulo finished telling them, they were silent a long moment. Finally, Qi'ra said, "I'm sorry that happened to you."

But she didn't feel all that sorry. At least he'd had parents. His datapad, brought all the way from Coruscant, was by far the most valuable possession of any of the White Worms. He'd been given an education. Enough to eat during his most formative years. Qi'ra would have cut off a finger for a past like that.

But Tsuulo took her words at face value. "Thanks," he said. It was one of the few words he could pronounce in Basic.

He stood and stretched, bleeping out something.

Han said, "He says he'll take the first watch shift. While he's out there, he'll make good on our word to Beejay and strip Reezo's speeder."

"Come wake one of us up in a few hours," Qi'ra said as Tsuulo pushed aside the fuselage scrap and stepped into the night.

She and Han were alone now.

"I should have let you drive," she said, all in a rush. "I was wrong to insist on doing it myself. I'd read about it and talked about it, and I thought that meant I could do it, but . . . I don't have a *feel* for it the way you do."

His eyes narrowed, and he studied her for a long moment. "You're . . . different," he said at last.

The power of anger swelled behind her eyes, and she glared blaster bolts right back at him. "Let me guess," she began scathingly. "I'm not like other girls?" She knew a pickup line when she heard it. Somehow, she was disappointed to discover that Han was just like all the rest.

"No, I mean you're not like other *people*. That's the second time you've admitted you were wrong about something."

She blinked, her anger fleeing as quickly as it came. "Oh." Then: "Really? That's . . . different?"

He shrugged. "Most people argue just to argue. But not you. When you're wrong, you just come out and say it."

Qi'ra considered this. "It would be deeply impractical to continue on the wrong path just for the sake of argument."

His lips turned up into a half smile. "And you're never impractical."

"I try not to be."

Han rubbed at his eyes. Maybe he was getting tired after all. His ruddy brown hair was curling slightly at the nape now that it was dry, and something mud-like was streaked across his right cheek. She considered whether to draw his attention to it but decided not to.

"Speaking of practical," he said, and Qi'ra had a funny feeling he was going to ask a question she didn't like. "Why here? All the way across town? This is the worst part of Coronet City, and it's so far away from the White Worm den, I imagine you can't make it out here very often."

She said nothing. He wanted more of her secrets. More of *her*.

"What I mean is," he continued, "it just doesn't seem practical. How did you find this place anyway? What were you doing way out here in the freighter boneyard?"

Wind whistled through the tree outside. Bilgefrogs croaked out that dawn was not too far away. A clanking sound nearly sent Qi'ra out of her chair, but Han said, "That was Tsuulo. I bet he just removed the holo-flames attachment."

She settled back, placed her hands on the table. Her short nails were grimed with dirt.

Finally, she said, "I grew up here. In the Silo."

Han's eyes flew wide.

"So I knew the territory, knew about the boneyard.

Mostly, I think I keep a safe house here because I want to always remember where I came from. I want a reminder, every time I'm eating rat sludge for breakfast or pick-pocketing an innocent person for Lady Proxima, that things used to be worse. If they can get better once, they can get better again, right?"

Han was studying her closely, almost like he was seeing her for the first time. And she didn't hate it.

"That makes sense," he said carefully. "Is it true what they say about the Silo? That it's Corellian hell?"

"It's worse," she said, and her voice sounded empty and hollow even to her own ears.

"How so?"

"Actually . . . I'd rather not talk about that."

"Suit yourself," he said, but she could tell he was disappointed.

"Let's talk about that speeder instead," she said, if only to change the subject. "You were awfully familiar with that garage. And you knew just what to say to that droid to convince her to let us go."

Han scratched at the smear on his face, then pulled his fingers away in dismay. "Ugh," he said. "I hope that's mud."

"The droid?" Qi'ra prompted.

"Beejay," Han said. "She's a mechanical repair droid.

Someone repurposed her to help build custom speeders. She's quite good, knows a lot. I've learned from her. You know she has her own speeder too? Bee is kind of obsessed with the idea of building the perfect custom speeder. She thinks she's going to win a race herself someday."

"And she hates Reezo's speeder."

"*Hates*. With the rage of an exploding sun. All those useless attachments. There's nothing more offensive to Bee than a customization that does not specifically"—Han modulated his voice to sound mechanical and female— "*optimize performance and increase efficiency*." He grinned. "The speeder she's working on is the ugliest in the garage, but when she's done, it'll have it where it counts."

Qi'ra's brain was finally catching up to the fact that her body was exhausted. She yawned and stretched, saying, "So that's where you've been going after shift every night. To work on your own speeder."

His face was suddenly stricken; Han was terrible at keeping his feelings hidden. "You won't tell anyone, will you?"

"Not anyone," Qi'ra said. And she meant it. Unless he betrayed her in some way. Or if she really needed the leverage. But *probably* she wouldn't tell anyone. "You pilot the way a fish swims in water," she observed. "You're a natural."

"I've done a little driving for Proxima," he said. "Some getaway stuff. But not much."

"You should do more of it. Practice. On the other hand, maybe I should never drive a speeder again."

"I'm glad you're bad at driving," he said.

"*What?*"

"I'm glad there's something in the galaxy you aren't instantly good at. You might be the smartest, most competent person I've ever met."

Qi'ra narrowed her eyes at him. Was he flirting with her? Han could turn an insult into a compliment as smoothly as he took those hairpin turns. No wonder he was a finalist for the Head position. Lady Proxima could make use of a slick talker like him.

No, he wasn't flirting, she decided. He was acknowledging her worth from a place of genuine respect. Not something she was used to.

"How did you end up with the White Worms?" she asked. Time to put *him* on the spot for once.

Han ran a hand through his mussed brown hair. "I . . . I was on the street for a long time, running with gangs, doing odd jobs. I was glad when the White Worms took me in."

"Parents?" she prodded. "A secret education, like Tsuulo?"

He opened his mouth, closed it. Then: "My old man was a lost prince, seventh in line to the throne of Hovea Nuket IV. He ran away when his family refused to bless his marriage to a dancing girl."

Qi'ra blinked. "Liar."

Han just grinned.

"How old are you?" Qi'ra asked.

He shrugged. "How should I know? When you're on the streets, the time sort of blends together."

Qi'ra laughed.

"What's so funny?"

"I have no idea how old I am either. Eighteen-ish? Maybe? I've stopped growing, is all I can say."

"That's my best guess too," he said. "Eighteen-ish."

"So, back to your father. I take it you didn't get along?"

He shrugged. "Sometimes. I remember one night after he'd been drinking, he took me back to the freighter factory where he worked. We just sat on the fence, staring at the shipyard full of fancy new ships. He sipped his bottle of ale and kicked at the fence, and I remember it was getting really cold. So I asked him why he'd dragged me all the way out there, and he said, 'I wanted you to see this. These ships. This is what I build. What I give to the galaxy. But no matter how many hours I put in, I'm nothing, a nobody.'" Han paused in the telling and looked her straight in the eye. "Then he said, 'Han, my boy, when you grow up, don't build ships like me. You're meant for better. You're meant to *fly* them.'"

Qi'ra didn't know what to say. "That's . . . that's really . . . Wait. Are you lying again?"

"I guess you'll never know." At her frown he added hastily: "I'll tell you one true thing, Qi'ra, something I haven't told anyone, just because you told me about the Silo."

"I'm listening."

"The reason I want my own speeder, the reason I work so hard on it, risk so much for it." He took a deep breath. "It's the closest I'll ever get to flying a starship."

At last, something rang true. "I guess I can understand that. But did you or did you not run away from your parents?" she pressed.

Han avoided looking at her. "Actually, I'd rather not talk about that."

She waited the space of three heartbeats. "Han," she said softly, and his gaze snapped to hers. "It's okay to have things you never want to talk about. Like I do."

Some kind of understanding passed between them. It wasn't a practical feeling, but she felt it the same way she would feel a fist in the gut. Or maybe a whispered breath on her ear.

"Yeah," he said, nodding slowly. "It's okay."

After another moment of comfortable silence, he added, "You know, I think I'll be able to sleep now."

"Me too," she said.

She had two tattered, stained blankets on the shelf. She gave one to Han, who stretched out on the table and pillowed his head on his bent arm. Within moments, his chest fell and rose with the deep, even breathing of sleep.

Qi'ra laid down on her cot and pulled the other blanket up to her chin. Her last thought was that a boy she hardly knew had come into this place she never shared with anyone, was in fact sleeping beside her, and she was glad he was here.

CHAPTER 10

It felt like only moments had passed when Tsuulo woke Han to take a watch shift, and a few hours after that, when the sun was rising in an uncharacteristically clear sky, Han finally woke Qi'ra.

"Already?" she said, yawning and stretching.

"It's daytime out there," he whispered so as not to wake Tsuulo, who was curled up on the table, the blanket kicked down to his feet. "Maybe we should get going?"

"No, get some sleep," Qi'ra said, rising. "We're safe here for a while. Rest while you can. I'll keep watch and come up with a plan."

So that's what they did. Han was asleep again as soon as his head hit the cot, and he didn't stir until someone shook him awake.

"Han, get up, you lazy gwerp," Tsuulo said in Huttese. "Qi'ra needs our help."

Through sheer force of will, Han got to his feet. His muscles were stiff and sore, and his very bones ached. No surprise, since they'd been running all day and night with very little sleep or food.

Speaking of food . . . something smelled delicious. Qi'ra was at the table, and as he sat beside her, she handed him an eel skewer dripping with sauce. "I picked up some food for us this afternoon."

"It's afternoon?" he said. He grabbed his skewer and bit down. Sauce dripped down his chin, and he caught it with a finger, not wanting to waste a single drop. It didn't taste particularly good, but it was better than the White Worm breakfast sludge, and he needed the energy it would provide. "With what money?" he asked with his mouth full.

"I always keep a few credits hidden here," she said. "When I can."

Light trickled into the space around the sorry excuse for a door and through an air vent above their heads. A few things about Qi'ra's safe house had escaped his notice in the dark. Like the dried flowers sticking out of an old soup can on the shelf. The ratty cargo blanket that someone had embroidered with swirls of blue thread. And hanging above the head of the cot, a chandelier of sorts, made of old wire and bits of colored glass.

Qi'ra loved this place, and she loved beautiful things. Gruffly, he said, "Tsuulo said you needed our help."

"I've figured out how we can get back into town," she said. "But I'm not sure where to go next or what we should do. I need your help deciding our next move."

"I know what we should do," Han said. "Run away to Kor Vella. We could get lost in that city, easy. No one there knows us."

"Is running away your answer to everything?" Qi'ra said.

Han frowned. "I never run away from a fight. Well," he amended, "unless I'm pretty sure I'm going to die."

"Anyway, I've no doubt our descriptions are all over Kor Vella too," she said. "They might not know about Tsuulo yet." She indicated the Rodian with a lift of her chin. He sat at the other end of the table, fiddling with something he'd yanked off the speeder. "But you and I will be spotted the moment we're out in the open."

"So what do you suggest?" Han asked.

"We need more information before we can decide anything. About that datacube. About why everyone wants it so badly. Your friend Tool tossed it to you, said to run for your life. That means he trusts you."

"He might not be functional anymore," Han pointed out. He didn't like the way saying that made him feel. "Last I saw him, he was getting blasted."

"What about the people he worked for? I think if we contacted them, let them know that Tool entrusted the datacube to you for a reason, they'd be forced to listen to us. They might extend some trust to us too."

The same wind that had blown the clouds from

the Corellian skies rattled the fuselage scrap that covered their doorway. Icy air gusted against Han's cheeks. Tsuulo looked up from his project and said, "Finding the Droid Gotra is a better idea than tangling with a smuggling syndicate or the Empire. And even though none of *them* are looking for me, Lady Proxima has figured out by now that I'm helping you. So my vote is to contact Tool or his employer."

"What did he say?" asked Qi'ra

"He votes we contact the Droid Gator."

"Fine. How?"

Han rubbed at his chin. "Tool might still be alive."

"Even if he's not," Tsuulo said, "I might be able to pull something from his memory banks or salvage his comm, find out who he communicated with last."

The thought of sifting through the dead metal shell that used to be his friend made the eel skewer sit poorly in Han's belly. "I guess," he said, and relayed Tsuulo's words to Qi'ra.

"It would be a huge risk, going back to the Foundry," she said.

Han shrugged, "Maybe we'll get lucky."

"I'll ask the Force for its blessing," Tsuulo said.

Han took the last bite of skewer, wiped his mouth with his sleeve, and said, "You sure that's how the Force works?"

Tsuulo slumped in his chair. "No."

"Then why—?"

The spines on his head fluttered. "I don't know any-thing, okay? No one will tell me anything about it! No one knows. . . ." He swallowed hard, as if collecting himself. "There was this fellow who always loitered at a street corner near where I lived. Wore dirty robes, long beard; he was always preaching, handing out pamphlets. One day I finally took one. It led me to an underground museum in Coruscant. Everything there was illegal, and I shouldn't have gone, but I was just a kid, barely twelve years old. I looked around. They had this book—well, an ancient manuscript—called the *Annals of Light and Being*. I read every page that was on display, and it just . . . made sense. It was like my eyes were opened, and I knew the Force was real."

"What's he talking about, Han?" Qi'ra asked.

"Converting to some religion."

"Then, a couple of years later, Imperials found out about the museum. They raided the place. The owner disappeared. The street preacher disappeared. The *Annals* disappeared. No one would tell me what happened to them, and no one could answer my questions about the Force. But I know it's real. I don't know how it works, but it helps me. Every day. I can *feel* it."

"What's he saying?"

"He's talking about his feelings."

"Ew," she said.

"Listen, pal, I don't care if you pray to a Force or a god or whatever. Can't hurt, right?" Han expected a look of gratitude or something for his being so gracious.

Instead, Tsuulo's one good antenna drooped with disappointment. "Sure," he said. "Can't hurt."

"So about the Foundry," Qi'ra said. "It's a risk, but not so risky as continuing to fly blind. I say we go for it. See if we can find Tool, make contact with the Droid Gotra."

There were so many reasons not to do it. The Kaldana thugs could be waiting for him. He could be faced with Tool's nonfunctioning carcass. It was too near White Worm territory.

But Qi'ra was right; they were flying blind, and that was going to get them killed faster than anything.

"I agree. Tsuulo?"

"I agree."

Han looked to Qi'ra. "You have a plan for getting us there?"

"I do. I thought about it all night."

This ought to be good. "So let's hear it."

Qi'ra smiled, that enormous smile that was like the sun bursting through Corellian clouds. "We take the speeder."

Han and Tsuulo gaped at her. "That's it? All night, and that's what you came up with?"

"Hey, a big part of figuring out the perfect plan is eliminating all the *bad* plans," she said. "And I can assure you, I thoroughly examined and discarded at least ten alternate possibilities."

"But that speeder is bright green!" he protested. "With Rodian antennae! Not exactly the best way to lay low. Everyone who sees that thing is going to remember it."

"Yeah, we'll have to take off the antennae. For now!" she added hastily when Tsuulo started to rise from the table. "We can reattach them later. You can do that, right?"

Tsuulo mumbled that he could.

"Reezo is probably looking everywhere for his speeder," Han said. "Bee has freed him from the engine compartment by now, and it's a good bet he's mad as hell. And out for revenge."

She shrugged. "It's not like he'll go to CorSec for help locating an illegal vehicle, right? And he's looking for his Rodian speeder, driven by his Rodian brother. Now that most of the customizations have been stripped, we'll be in a normal speeder, driven by you. Well, almost normal. It will still be bright green. But this is Corellia. Everyone customizes their speeder a little. We'll blend right in."

Han considered this and found a flaw in her reasoning. "You said descriptions of us are planetwide now, even as far as Kor Vella. We're sure to be recognized."

"We'll have to wear hoods," she conceded. "I was going to send Tsuulo into the Bottoms' market to pick up a few cloaks. We'll wear driving goggles too."

"How will we pay for the cloaks and goggles?"

Tsuulo held up the project he was working on. "Bounce package," the Rodian said. "I've modified it to work on droids and personal lifts as well as speeders. I'll sell it in the market and buy some cloaks."

Han was a little sorry to see the bounce package go. It had really saved their necks the night before, not to mention made him feel, if only for a moment, like he was flying. "You've thought this through," he said.

"I have."

They could keep running, but everything would eventually catch up to them. They needed to fix this, and in order to do that, they had to know more. "All right. Fine," he said. "We'll just drive right up to the Foundry like we belong there. When in doubt, brazen it out, right?"

A few hours later they were cloaked and goggled and speeding toward the Foundry. The sun was already low in the sky; they'd let Han sleep in a bit, and gathering their new clothes had taken some time. It would have been nice if they could have afforded some fresh water for bathing too, but you couldn't have everything.

"We'll get there right on time for shift change," Qi'ra explained.

"We don't have employee identichips," Tsuulo pointed out. "We can't just walk right in."

"Sure we can," Han said, steering into a busy thoroughfare. No one gave them a second glance. So far, so good. "I've walked into the Foundry plenty of times. You just stand in the employment line. Each day they pick a bunch of people to do some work under the table. Mostly cleanup, sometimes testing. The pay is terrible, and if you're injured or killed, too bad for you. But it's a way in."

"How do we make sure we get picked?" Qi'ra asked.

Han smiled at her. "Trust me."

"Something's wrong," Tsuulo said.

"What do you mean?" Han asked.

Tsuulo pointed to a group of stormtroopers marching through a fish market. "And there." He pointed to a droid walking into an apartment building. "That's a *maintenance* droid, and it's carrying a blaster."

Qi'ra smacked Tsuulo's hand down. "Don't point," she said. "It will draw attention."

"But do you see?" he persisted. "There are more beings packing firepower today than I've ever seen since my family arrived on this awful planet."

"I see it," Qi'ra said. "I've been noticing it too." Han couldn't tell if she actually understood Tsuulo or if she put it together on a hunch. "We need to watch each other's backs going into the Foundry."

It took them less than an hour to get past Old Town and into the manufacturing district. The Foundry was a huge complex of buildings. Smokestacks that stretched as high as skyscrapers belched dirty smoke. Freighters took off and landed in the distance, hauling recently manufactured components through the Foundry's small, dedicated spaceport. Other components were hauled out on freight speeders; a line of them headed toward the outskirts of the city to the shipyards, where component parts would be assembled into all sorts of starships, but mostly light freighters.

Han parked their speeder in the designated area. Tsuulo pulled out his datapad and encrypted the console controls. A good encryption wasn't a guarantee against theft, but it would make amateurs and street thieves think twice.

The three of them kept their hoods up and their goggles on as they strode toward the massive metal gate and the line of ragged hopefuls waiting outside. There were hundreds of them, waiting to see if they'd get picked for work.

"You sure you can get us in?" Qi'ra asked.

"There are a lot more people than I expected," he admitted.

"Han!"

"Hey, we might get lucky," he said with a shrug.

Tsuulo began praying to the Force.

The sun was setting beyond the spaceport, taking the day's little warmth with it. Hopeful workers huddled close, hands stuffed in sleeves and pockets, hoods up, threadbare jackets clipped tight. Everyone was weathered and wrinkled, hungry and cold.

"See, we've had some luck already," Han whispered as they got in line. "This cold snap gives us a good reason to keep these cloaks on. And our driving goggles look like safety eyewear."

Qi'ra gave him a look that could curdle milk.

A klaxon sounded, signaling end of shift. A moment later, the gate slid open and exhausted workers poured out, anxious to get home for the night. After the flood of beings became a mere trickle, it was followed by a group of humans in stiff blue uniforms. One woman held a datapad; a man carried a portable loudhailer.

The fellow with the loudhailer held it up and shouted,

"We're looking for some duct rats tonight. Volunteers please step forward."

A murmur rose from the crowd and everyone shifted in place. Fully a third of the supplicants turned and left.

"I take it no one wants to be a 'duct rat'?" Qi'ra whispered to Han.

"It's the worst job in the Foundry," he whispered back. Then he stepped forward, and Qi'ra and Tsuulo followed.

Over a hundred volunteers remained. The woman with the datapad pointed at a few and told them to go home. "Too big," she said. "We need small bodies for small spaces."

Han pushed his friends forward. "I've got some small bodies right here," he called out. Then he bent his knees and hunched a little, trying to look slighter. "We're experienced crawlers. We'll get those ducts clean for you."

The man with the loudhailer waved them through.

They hurried toward the entrance before anyone could change their minds or get a better look at them.

"We did it!" Qi'ra said.

"I told you we'd get lucky," Han said.

"The Force heard my prayers," Tsuulo said. Han rolled his eyes.

"So what are duct rats anyway?" Qi'ra asked.

"Beings who crawl around the air vents and machinery intakes, cleaning them of ash and soot, chemical residue, the occasional life-form."

"And it's dangerous?" she asked.

"Yeah, it's really easy to take a wrong turn and find yourself in the intake of a live machine. And sometimes people get a bad cough—the killing kind."

"Why don't they use droids?"

"The particulates tend to gum up their joints, among other things. Besides, good droids are expensive. It's easier and cheaper to just use desperate people."

They reached the entrance, where a Kel Dor stood sentry, his breather mask wheezing with age and grime. "We're here for duct cleaning duty," Han said. "Which way?"

The Kel Dor opened the door for them, revealing a massive, bustling assembly floor, but he pointed right toward a branching hallway. The three of them strode into the factory.

"I can't believe that worked," Qi'ra said.

"Me neither," Han muttered.

"What?"

"I said, I told you it would."

Qi'ra lowered her voice. "Now we need a distraction. So we can slip away to the basement."

The air was hot and dry, a welcome change from outside at first, but within moments, Han felt sweat breaking out on his neck. Everything smelled of smoke and overheated lubricant, all tinged with a sharp metallic bite. Parts clanked and conveyer belts groaned. Stamping presses crashed down on metal sheets, and drill bits screamed holes into stubborn joists. Mechanical arms set in ceiling mounts moved blindingly fast, sorting and tagging, dropping adhesive here, trimming away excess there. Through it all, a flock of droids and organics checked equipment, supervised conveyers, cleaned metal shavings and black oil from the floor.

Everyone was haggard and dazed, going through the motions on autopilot. Han didn't see a single smile or hear a word of conversation. Many were missing fingers or limbs. One Besalisk fellow had a constellation of burn scars across his cheek; he'd obviously gotten a face full of hot metal shavings.

The Foundry was a joyless, luckless place, and for the thousandth time, Han was glad he'd joined the White Worms instead of embracing the factory life.

"Han? Any idea for a distraction?" Qi'ra prompted. "We could *accidentally* crash one of these conveyers. See that guy pushing the janitor cart?"

She was pointing to a human male, no older than

they were, pushing a large cart full of scrap. He paused occasionally to sweep something up. When his cart was full, he'd take it to the smelter.

She said, "We could spill the scrap onto the belt where they're making those . . . thingies. . . ."

"Alluvial dampers."

"Whatever. All those shavings and scrap bits would stop the conveyer in its tracks, right?"

"Right," Tsuulo said. "But then we'd—"

A scream erupted, overpowering the noise of the factory. Then came a heartrending keen that made the hair on the back of Han's neck stand up straight. Everyone on the assembly floor left their posts to congregate around something.

A red light came on, pulsing from the ceiling high above, and an emergency siren flooded their ears.

What was that? Qi'ra mouthed, but Han couldn't hear her over the sound of the siren.

Han smelled blood. A moment later, bodies parted and Han glimpsed a man lying on the floor in a pool of crimson, clutching at his empty elbow socket. His severed forearm lay stiff beside him.

"That's our distraction," Han said in her ear. "Let's go! The basement is this way."

Han hastened them down the side of the building

toward the back, where an access corridor would lead them to a freight lift. "I guess we got lucky again," he said.

"Our luck was that man's loss," Tsuulo pointed out. "The great philosopher Flayshil Crena speculates that luck is a finite thing, to be doled out in increments. Maybe the galaxy's luck will run out someday."

"Tsuulo, remind me to never get an education," Han said.

"Better him than us," Qi'ra said, and even though Han agreed with her, it didn't quite sit right.

They reached the corridor, turned right, and came to a turbolift. Han was about to activate the console when the doors slid open and a tall white-haired man wearing a management uniform strode out.

"*Blast*," Qi'ra whispered.

"What are you doing here?" he demanded. Then his head cocked as he recognized the siren wailing in the next building.

"Uh . . . some guy lost an arm back there," Han said. "Blood went everywhere. Conveyer belt got gummed up, threw alluvial damper parts all over the floor, knocked a few people in the head. The shift supervisor sent us to grab all the cleaning and medical supplies we can carry."

Qi'ra added, "He said there's a supply closet this way?"

Han resisted the urge to kick her. When lying, it was always best to keep your embellishments to a minimum.

But the white-haired man thumbed toward the lift. "Down two levels, out the door and to your right. Hells, really? The alluvial damper line? We haven't had a dismemberment on that line for almost two years."

And with that he strode away without giving them a second glance.

"That could have gone very badly," Qi'ra said, staring after him.

"But it didn't!"

She narrowed her eyes at Han. "You're very good at talking your way out of things." It didn't sound like a compliment.

And that rankled, because maybe he wanted it to be. A little respect from her shouldn't be so hard. Not that her opinion mattered. It wasn't like she was his friend or anything.

Tsuulo directed the lift to the basement level, which turned out to be a damp, cluttered storage space for old assembly works. It reminded Han a little of the White Worm lair, with its defunct machines and rusty pipes and everywhere the slick sheen of seeping water.

"This way," Han said, and he took them to the door that he knew led into the underground bunker, the one where Tool had been shot while throwing the datacube to him. "Be ready for anything," he said, and he keyed the door open.

The sick-sweet scent of carrion nearly overpowered them.

"What in holy moons is that?" Tsuulo said, waving a hand in front of his face.

"Dead body," Han said. "So watch your step."

The room was pitch-black; all that blaster fire must have destroyed the lighting.

"We have to close the door behind us," Qi'ra whispered. She was right on his heels. "We *have* to."

"I'll fire up my datapad," Tsuulo offered, and sure enough within moments their way was lit by a soft blue glow.

Qi'ra closed the door while Han took stock. The floor was sticky with blood. Blaster marks scorched the walls. There was only one dead body; Han would never have recognized him except for the ridiculous mustache that still drifted down his face even in death. Mustache Guy was definitely the source of that awful smell. It had only been a little over a day, but he was in a ripe state of decomposition thanks to the Foundry's hot atmosphere— and the fact that blaster fire had ripped open his belly, spilling his guts on the floor. Tiny rodent paw prints smattered the floor around him.

"Poor fellow," came Qi'ra's voice.

Han had seen worse. Still, he had to look away. No sign of the Kaldana woman; she must have been one of the people who'd chased him into the sewer. "Tool?" he whispered. Tsuulo's datapad only lit the space around him, leaving the edges of the room in darkness.

Han heard—or maybe only thought he heard—a slight mechanical whirring.

"Tool?" he said again.

The sound came again, stretched out and slippery as if coming from a dying power source. "Haaaaan."

"Tool! Tsuulo, over here. Can you light this corner for me? I think he . . . Oh, hell."

Tool was crumpled on the floor, legs splayed, his back against the wall. His head drooped down to his chest, and his welder had broken off; it lay dismembered on the ground beside him. He was badly dented and covered in scorch marks, and the light indicator for his power core was dim, blinking out at irregular intervals.

"Haaaaan," Tool said, his voice garbled and scratched. "Need reeepaaaair."

"Help me turn him over!" Han ordered. "I need to open his access compartment." Qi'ra and Tsuulo bent to help.

They grunted and heaved, but Tool hardly budged. "This is the oldest droid I've ever seen," Tsuulo said, catching his breath. "He has a fusion power core! That's ancient! I bet a collector would pay top credits for—"

"Less talking, more lifting," Han said as they tried again.

This time, they managed to get him onto his shoulder. Han ripped open the access compartment in his back and rerouted all the power from his legs and attachments to his receptors and memory banks.

"That's exactly how I would have done it," Tsuulo said.

"Sorry, pal," Han said to Tool. "This will leave you paralyzed for now, but at least you'll be able to talk to us."

"Could not move anyway," Tool said, and Han was relieved to hear the clarity in his voice. "A blaster severed the central servomotor cable in my back. I was helpless even to reroute power. I'm very glad you came when you did."

"We can fix you up," Han assured him.

"His fusion core shut down due to overheating," Tsuulo said, peering into the compartment. "He's been on auxiliary power all day. Once the core cools off, I can get it humming again. Tool, is it all right with you if my datapad talks to your internal processor? It's the fastest way for me to run a diagnostic."

"Please do," Tool said. "But I will thank you to stay

out of my memory banks. I assume you came to get more information about that datacube. Do you still have it, Han, does it remain intact?"

"I have it. Well, Tsuulo does. It's intact," Han assured him.

"And we *do* need information," Qi'ra said. "Will you help us?"

Tool cocked his head, as if his photoreceptors weren't working quite right. "Ah, yes, the girl. Everyone is looking for you too. I heard a lot of chatter about you both on the holonet before my fusion core powered off."

"Why?" Qi'ra pleaded. "Why does everyone want to kill us over that thing?"

"Oh that is nice," Tool said flatly. "Very nice what a relief."

"I'm powering your coolant system with my datapad," Tsuulo said. "But once your fusion core is running, I'll need a recharge in return."

"Of course."

"The datacube?" Qi'ra prompted. "There's a dead guy with cooked intestines on the floor over there because of it, and I want to know why."

Han put a hand on her shoulder. "Easy, Qi'ra." Once she was on a mission, it was all she thought about. She was like one of Rebolt's hounds with a biscuit. Sometimes, that could be a good thing. But other times, like now, you had to feel your way through a situation. And Tool was not going to talk easily, especially if Qi'ra bludgeoned him with questions.

To the droid, he said, "You're not supposed to talk about it, are you?"

"I am not."

"This is very important to you."

"It is."

"You threw the cube to me, remember? Because you trust me. Which turned out to be a smart move. I'm back, and the cube is fine."

"What are you going to do with it?" Tool asked.

"That's why we need your help. Without more information, we don't know what to do."

"Wow," said Tsuulo, sifting through the data on his pad. "You've made a lot of improvements. You're like an illegal street speeder. Ugly on the outside, but full of surprises."

Han could swear that Tool was beaming with pleasure. "Thank you," the droid intoned.

"The cube?" Qi'ra prodded. "Tool, what do you think we should do with it?"

"Give it to the Droid Gotra of course. We won that bid fair and square."

She took a deep breath. "Okay, let's start there. What is the Droid Gotra?"

Tool said nothing.

"I have something that might change your mind about talking to us," said Tsuulo, pulling a big metal lump out of his pocket.

"What is that?" Tool asked.

"This," Tsuulo said, "is a holo-flames attachment." He flicked a switch, its tiny projectors lit up, and flames danced all through the room, lighting the walls in dreamlike blue. The blood on the floor glinted slickly.

"Oh," said Tool. "My."

"I could program it to contour itself to your shape."

"I don't know of any other droids who have one," Tool said.

"You'd be one of a kind," Han assured him.

Suddenly, Tool couldn't talk fast enough.

CHAPTER 11

Qi'ra couldn't believe their luck. First they'd just walked right into the Foundry. Then Han had smooth-talked his way past that manager at the turbolift. And just now Tsuulo had figured out the perfect way to get Tool to talk. Things like that never happened to her.

Things like that never happened to her *when she was alone*, she corrected herself. But strangely, unexpectedly, she and Han and Tsuulo were turning out to be a good team.

"The Droid Gotra," Tool said, "is an organization dedicated to droid emancipation."

"It's a *terrorist* organization," Tsuulo said. "Everyone on Coruscant—"

"You are a victim of Imperial propaganda," Tool said. "The Droid Gotra has occasionally gone to extreme measures, certainly, but we want nothing more than peace and freedom for ourselves, just like any sentient species."

Tool's voice was completely devoid of inflection, which Qi'ra found unsettling. You could tell a lot about a person by how they talked. In fact, she hadn't realized how much she counted on inflection and tone to read a situation until it was gone. "You must be a powerful group," Qi'ra pointed out, "to bid a billion credits for something."

"That bid stretched our resources," Tool admitted. "But it would have been worth it. We started as a loosely connected group of battle droids, beings who were abandoned after the Clone Wars or repurposed against their will for other functions. But now our organization is large, consisting of all manner of droids, even a few organic sympathizers. We have been working to establish a cell here on Corellia."

Qi'ra righted one of the chairs and sat in it, turning her back to the mustached corpse. "So you're a droid with a cause," she said. There was nothing more dangerous than a true believer.

"The cause of droid equality is the most important in the galaxy," he said. His words were passionate, but his tone was as emotionless as if he'd said, *Please pass the rat porridge.* To Tsuulo, Tool added, "I think we'll be able to reactivate my fusion core soon."

Tsuulo made a noise of agreement.

"So why did the Gotra want this cube so badly? We know it's Imperial shield generator tech, created by someone called the Engineer. But we can't read the blueprints. Not even Tsuulo over there can make heads or tails of them."

"Heads or tails," Tool intoned. "I will add that to my repertoire immediately."

At Qi'ra's confused look, Han explained: "He recently uploaded some programming that allows him to speak in clichés."

"Metaphors," Tool corrected.

"That's what I mean," Han said.

The way Han hovered over his flat-voiced friend was . . . interesting. He really cared about that droid. He had moved so fast, so unerringly, to get inside Tool's innards and rewire him before he deactivated. Han was a handy guy to have around in a tough situation, she had to admit.

"You were about to tell us about the shield tech?" she prodded.

"You are correct," Tool said. "It is a blueprint for a shield generator. A very special shield generator."

"How so?" Han asked. Content that his friend was safe in Tsuulo's capable hands, Han pulled up the chair beside Qi'ra and sat.

"It has very low energy requirements," Tool explained. "Even the smallest freighters or personal yachts could make use of it at a low cost."

"That's not worth a billion credits," Qi'ra pointed out.

"I am not finished," Tool said. "It's also portable. In other words, you can disconnect it and lug it from ship to ship."

"You mean it's not hardwired into the ship itself," Han said.

"It is not."

"But it works just as well as any other deflector shield?" The skepticism in Han's voice was obvious.

"Han, my boy," Tool said. "It's military grade. Able to deflect even low-ordnance proton torpedoes."

Han whistled.

"Now do you see," Tool said. "The Empire has a near monopoly on shipped goods, but this technology puts freighter and cruiseliner deflector shielding on par with that of a Star Destroyer. All for a fraction of the price. Small freight companies could actually make a living again."

"And honest smugglers," Han noted.

Tsuulo said something, and Han translated: "It's a great equalizer, Tsuulo says. It puts droids on the same level playing field as organics."

"Playing field," Tool repeated, no doubt adding the metaphor to his repertoire. "Yes, it levels up the playing field."

Qi'ra didn't think that "levels up" was quite the right idiom, but she let it go. Her mind was churning with the new data and its ramifications. "That's why the Kaldana Syndicate wanted it so badly," she mused aloud. "With this kind of shield tech, there'd be no end to their piracy. They could take on bigger ships with more firepower. They'd become the richest syndicate in the galaxy. Bigger than the Crimson Dawn or the Pykes. Maybe even more powerful than the Hutts."

"Yes."

"Lady Proxima has no use for it," Qi'ra continued. "No doubt her intent was to resell it at a higher price."

"This is a smart young woman you have here," Tool said to Han.

Han said, "I know."

Qi'ra bristled. "Nobody *has* me."

"I know that too," Han said.

Still glaring at him, she said, "But where did the cube come from? And why is some of it still encrypted? Who . . ." Frustration was causing her voice to rise, which was the last thing they needed. She glanced nervously at the door they'd come through, hoping it was fairly soundproof. Qi'ra took a deep breath and said in little more than a whisper: "Who is the Engineer?"

"I don't know her name," Tool said. "No one does. Just that she is an Imperial defector. She was involved in a huge secret project for the Empire. The Engineer designed the deflector shield for them, but when she was done, she realized the value of her creation and fled, plans in hand. Her intent is to sell them to the highest bidder and retire anonymously and with great wealth to one of the Outer Rim planets. Naturally, she came here to the center of the galaxy's shipbuilding industry, looking for buyers."

Qi'ra was silent a moment, considering. She noticed Han staring at her.

"What?"

He looked away quickly. "Nothing. It's just . . . I like that."

"You like what?"

"When your face"—he made a vague gesture with his hand—"does that thing. It gets thinky."

What in holy moons did that mean?

Tsuulo asked Tool a question, but Qi'ra only caught the word for "power."

"Yes, I am ready," Tool replied.

There was a slight hum, a few beeps. Tool's carapace jerked as if coming to life.

Tsuulo twittered something else, and Han shot forward out of the chair. "I want to watch!" he said. "The servomotor cable looked like it was in pretty bad shape to me. If you can rig it to work, I want to see how." For a guy who didn't want an education, Han sure seemed eager to learn.

While the boys knocked heads peering into Tool's access compartment, Qi'ra said, "Tool, tell me about the auction. Why did it go so wrong?"

"It's clear the Kaldana Syndicate had decided they were going to attain the merchandise no matter what," Tool said. "They are hateful, mechanophobic bigots who would rather start a galactic incident than let droids acquire advantageous tech. So when the Droid Gotra won the bid, they started firing, hoping to take the cube by force, or at least keep me from handing it over to my superiors."

"But you threw it to Han instead."

"He is a good kid," Tool said. "And he knows the sewers like the back of his hand. That is a ridiculous metaphor, by the way. I've never observed humans studying the backs of their hands."

"The Kaldana went after him hard," Qi'ra said. "We still might die because of this."

"You are angry I put Han at risk," Tool said.

"Yes," Qi'ra said.

Han grinned. "She cares about me."

"Don't flatter yourself. I'm angry on behalf of all of us," Qi'ra clarified.

"It was an easy choice," Tool said. "If the Kaldana got

their hands on that tech, it would put a stranglehold on Corellia's already sputtering economy. So it's better for the whole system, and it's better for the cause of droid equality, to keep it away from them. Of course I'm willing to sacrifice a few organics for all that."

Han was giving Tool a funny look, like he felt betrayed. Qi'ra didn't know what Han had expected. Of course Tool considered him expendable. Just like Lady Proxima. Everyone always stabbed everyone else in the back, when the circumstances were right.

Tsuulo bleated out something. Han said, "He wants to know about the encryption."

"Oh, right," Qi'ra said. "Tool, those plans are encrypted. Getting a hold of the datacube isn't going to help anyone."

"You are correct," the droid said. "The Engineer had agreed to contact the winning bidder and give them the encryption key. But as you know, the deal went bad. I'm sure the Kaldana believe they can crack the encryption with time and resources, and maybe they can."

Qi'ra reviewed what she knew. "So the Kaldana want to steal the cube. The Droid Gotra want it back so they can complete the transaction and get the encryption key. And Lady Proxima wants it so she can mark it up and resell it. And all of them want us dead."

"You forgot the Empire," Tool said. "They want it

back too. I'm not certain they know about you three yet, but based on the chatter I'm hearing over the holonet, they've managed to track their prodigal engineer here to Corellia."

Tsuulo swore.

Han said, "Yeah, we noticed there were a lot more stormtroopers hanging around these days."

Qi'ra was developing a strong opinion about what to do next.

"Please give the cube to me," Tool said.

But it was not that.

"The Droid Gotra won the bid," he added. "Let us complete the deal as agreed."

"No way," Qi'ra said. "The White Worms and the Kaldana would never forgive us. We'd have bounties on our heads for the rest of our short lives."

Tsuulo disengaged his datapad from the droid and closed Tool's access compartment. The Rodian boy stood and began chattering at them, waving his datapad in the air.

"Tsuulo votes for returning the data cube to the Engineer," Han said. "Starting over. That way, we're not stealing it from anyone; we're actually salvaging the deal."

That was exactly what Qi'ra had been thinking.

"But I'm not so sure," Han added. "I really don't like

the idea of that cube getting into Kaldana hands. Or the hands of any of the syndicates. If the deal starts all over, who knows which players would come to the table? The Droid Gotra might be the best option. I mean, it's for a good cause, right?"

Qi'ra stared at him. He'd said "Gotra" correctly for the first time, which meant he was deadly serious.

Tsuulo argued back, clearly disagreeing.

"Well, I don't know about the other droids," Han said, "but Tool is my friend, and he's no terrorist. I don't think he'd even be part of a group like that."

"If we salvage this deal," Qi'ra said, "the Gotra has a chance to come back and bid again. They might still end up with the cube. Since we're White Worms, Lady Proxima gets credit for making things right—that would take some heat off, yes? The Engineer ends up owing us a favor. I don't know about the Kaldana, but salvaging the deal gets at least a couple of groups off our backs."

Han rubbed at his jaw. He was exhausted; Qi'ra could see it in his eyes. "Our odds of survival would go way up," he said.

"I thought you didn't want to know the odds," Qi'ra said.

"Only *after* I've decided to do something," he said.

"If you agree," Tool said, "that you will not deliver the cube to the Kaldana or the White Worms, I will get word out through my contacts in the Gotra that you're interested in talking to the Engineer."

Qi'ra looked to Han, who nodded, then to Tsuulo, who said, "*Something* idea *somethingsomething* agree."

"All right," she said. "Let's do it."

"There," Tool said. "Already done." He had regained some mobility, so he leaned over and used a pincer extension to grab his dismembered welder from the floor.

"If we get out of this alive," Han said, "I can come back and reattach that for you."

"No need," Tool said. "My friends in the Gotra will handle it. They'll hook up the holo-flames enhancement too. We take good care of each other in the Gotra. We don't need organics at all anymore."

Something about that didn't sit right with Qi'ra, but there was no time to dwell on it because Tool said, "I just got an alert back. Imperial troops are approaching this facility."

Han and Qi'ra jumped to their feet as Tsuulo loosed a string of expletives.

"What do we do?" Qi'ra said. "My plan for getting out of here didn't include stormtroopers."

"Screw the plan," said Han. "We run like hell."

"No, wait. Tool said the Empire might not know about us. Tool, why are they here?"

The droid lumbered to his feet. He was even taller

than Qi'ra expected. No wonder they'd had such trouble heaving him onto his side. He listed to the left a little; it was clear that Tsuulo's patch to Tool's servomotor cable was merely that: a patch.

"I don't know for certain why they're here," Tool said, "but one possibility is they tracked the cube to this location, where the exchange went down."

Tsuulo threw his datapad into his pack and slung it over his shoulder. Han and Qi'ra pulled their goggles back on and flipped their hoods over their heads.

"Moloch and Rebolt are prowling the sewers," Han said. "They'll recognize us no matter what we're wearing. We can't go that way."

"On the other hand, if we go up top," Qi'ra added, "there's a chance everyone will think we're just normal factory workers."

"Turn right out of the lift," Tool said. "Follow the corridor to building three and exit out the south entrance. Building three houses the smelter; it's the most poorly guarded building in the Foundry complex. Organics and droids both hate being in that place."

"Thanks, Tool," Han said, already heading for the door, Qi'ra and Tsuulo close behind.

"Hurry," Tool called to their backs. "And you should know, the Engineer is not actually on Corellia."

Qi'ra spun back around. "What?"

"She has eyes on the ground—another ridiculous metaphor, the eyes would get stepped on and smashed if they were on the floor—but she would never risk landing. She's somewhere above the planet, ready to flee at a moment's notice. So if you want to meet with her, you'll have to go offworld."

Han gasped.

Qi'ra had no idea how to get offworld. Or how they would make contact with the Engineer in the first place. One thing at a time.

"C'mon!" She grabbed Han's sleeve and yanked him through the door.

CHAPTER 12

The skin of Han's face started to burn with heat even before they'd entered building three, with its resident smelter. Or maybe his cheeks were just warm from hearing those precious, golden words: *You'll have to go offworld.*

Han wasn't sure why the thought made his heart race, but it did.

Qi'ra reached the door first. It slid open, and hot air poured out, so hot it pushed her hair back. They stepped cautiously inside.

Tool was right; this building was not heavily guarded. Probably because no one came here if they could help it.

In the center of the room was a giant silo at least four stories high. Cartloads of scrap traveled on a conveyer toward the silo and up a steep ramp to the lip, where they were automatically tipped, emptied, then swiped to the side to make room for the next carts. Pipes along the ceiling fed the smelter with oxidation materials. From a round portal at the base of the silo poured glowing, molten ore in two streams—a wider one for good ore, a smaller one for slag.

The aqueducts bisected the building floor, traveling away from the smelter and under the wall, into another building. Han knew the liquid ore was cooled into sheets, which could be stamped and pressed and molded into all sorts of starship components.

He could guess where the slag aqueduct led: probably to the river and eventually the ocean. Dumping into the water was supposedly illegal on Corellia, but all the factories did it.

Workers stood on a catwalk above the molten rivers, using long prods to check for impurities. They wore shiny protective helmets and the thickest gloves Han had ever seen. They moved slowly and methodically, working in total silence, as though their hearts and minds were elsewhere. And they probably were. Factory workers used to make a decent living, but now that the Empire had nationalized shipbuilding, everyone was barely scraping by. Han guessed that most in this very room were involved in smuggling and black market trading, just to make ends meet.

Smuggling had become the only way for honest people to make a decent living around here. That meant Corellian lives were going to get even worse if the Kaldana pirates got ahold of that shield tech. Maybe giving it to the droids really was the right thing to do.

A droid with repulsorlift technology and multiple

dangling appendages floated around the side of the silo, checking gauges and making adjustments. Han wondered if it was part of the Gotra too. How far did their influence reach, exactly? How many members of the Droid Gotra were on Corellia now?

"Over there," Qi'ra said, pointing. "That's the door Tool mentioned."

It was all the way across the room. There were two ways to get there. One was to cross via the catwalk, which was occupied by workers who would most definitely sound the alarm if outsiders ran past. The other way to get there was by double-jumping over the aqueducts.

"It's not a bad jump," Tsuulo said, as if reading Han's thoughts. "Big leap, careful landing, small leap. Easy."

"Yeah," Han said. "Easy." Though, of course, if any of them misjudged it, they'd sink into liquid metal and burn alive. They wouldn't even have time to drown.

"I don't see any sentries," Qi'ra said. "But that droid up there might be a problem."

"We'll approach slow, then jump over the outtakes and sprint for the door," Han said.

"I say we take our chances with the smelter workers." Without waiting to see if he agreed, she began walking toward the catwalk stairs.

Han caught up to her, grabbed the sleeve of her cloak

and whipped her around. "Qi'ra, if one of them panics—"

The door behind them flew open. Han barely had time to register a sea of shiny white armor and heavy blasters before he was rushing headlong toward the molten streams. The footsteps of his friends followed close at his heels.

"Halt!" someone said, the voice filtered and mechanical. "You're wanted for questioning—"

Han leaped over the first aqueduct; his skin felt like it was on fire as he flew through the air. He landed hard, falling to his knees on purpose rather than allow his momentum to carry him right into the second aqueduct.

A body slammed into his back—Tsuulo!—pushing him forward. Han grappled at the edge of the second aqueduct to keep from toppling in. Heat seared his driving gloves, scalding his skin. Molten metal flowed and bubbled and spurted less than a meter from his face.

Hands yanked him back, saving him. "On your feet," Qi'ra ordered. She pulled at his arms until he got his legs under him.

Han expected to feel blaster fire in his back any second. Still, he paused to help Tsuulo gather his pack, which had slipped from the Rodian's shoulder. "Let's go!" he said, and the three of them leaped over the slag aqueduct and sprinted for the south exit.

A laser bolt exploded into the door ahead of them, leaving a huge blackened dent. They stopped in their tracks.

"I said *halt*," came the voice again. "Put your hands up."

Still facing their exit—and freedom—they did as asked, putting their hands in the air.

Qi'ra whispered, "What now, Improvise Guy?"

"Uh, I could use a good idea, Plan Everything Girl," he whispered back.

To their right, the workers on the catwalk had fallen to their knees, where they cowered, hands over their heads. The maintenance droid continued to whirl around the silo, oblivious to everything.

"Turn around, slowly," said the stormtrooper.

"Don't," Qi'ra said.

"Maybe we should cooperate—" Han started to say.

"If they were going to shoot us, they would have done it by now," she whispered back, low and fast. "They missed on purpose. They do *not* want us to go out that door, but they do want us alive and conscious."

The stormtrooper yelled, "I said turn around! Now!"

"Think we should make a run for it?" Han asked.

"Definitely."

Tsuulo said, "I'm not sure that door will open! It got hit hard."

"What did he say?" Qi'ra asked Han.

"He said run!"

As one, they burst forward, legs pumping as fast as they could go. Blaster fire erupted all around them. Han desperately hoped Qi'ra was right, that the stormtroopers were missing on purpose.

Tsuulo tried to palm the door open. It didn't budge.

He tried again. Another blast crashed into the wall near their heads. One of the workers screamed.

Han leaped forward and kicked the door as hard as he could. It groaned open, with a metal-scraping-metal sound Han felt deep in his throat.

The three of them exploded through the door and into the darkness of night and its open, icy air.

And right into the arms of five stormtroopers.

"Let me go!" Qi'ra yelled, clawing with hands and feet, while Tsuulo and Han tried to shake their own captors.

The barrel of a blaster pressed firm and cold into Han's temple. He went utterly still.

Blasters were similarly pointing at the others. Han watched as Qi'ra stopped fighting, took a quick, composing breath, and then stared straight ahead, hands folded in front of her. "Please don't shoot us," she said with preternatural calm. "We'll cooperate."

"Yes! What she said!" Han agreed. "We'll cooperate!"

One of the stormtroopers circled around to close the

door they'd just exited through, then took up a guard position. Leftward, toward building two, was a swath of paver lit by a flood light. The stormtroopers were not moving them into the light.

Something about all that was strange, but the blaster at Han's head made it hard to think.

Another stormtrooper stepped forward. He looked exactly the same as the others except for an orange pauldron on one shoulder.

"I have something for you," the stormtrooper said. And he held out an object to Qi'ra.

"What is it?" she asked, not moving to take it. The item was small, fitting easily in the palm of his gloved hand.

"A message, courtesy of the Engineer."

Han gasped.

Slowly, her eyes not leaving the stormtrooper's helmet, Qi'ra took the item from his hand.

"The Engineer has been watching you," he said. "She sends her regards, and she very much hopes you will be amenable to her message. Further, she hopes that you will not disseminate the *method* of the message's delivery, not ever, not to anyone."

With that, the stormtroopers pulled their blasters back, turned, and disappeared into the darkness.

"What just happened?" Han breathed.

Qi'ra stared down at the thing in her hand. "Seems like the Engineer still has secret friends among her former employer," she said. "It makes sense, I guess. She would never have defected without a solid plan. And that includes well-placed, loyal contacts. It's what I'd do."

"What did he give you?" Tsuulo asked, pointing to her hand.

"I think it's a holoprojector," she said.

"What does it say?" Tsuulo said, at the same moment Han said, "Well, turn it on!"

"Not yet," she replied, glancing around. They were at the edge of the Foundry complex, out of sight of any floodlights. "Those stormtroopers worked for the Engineer, but I'm sure more are on their way. We need to get under cover."

For the first time, Han felt that they might have a chance of getting out of this mess alive. The Engineer had contacted them! In a way that proved she was even more powerful than they'd realized. She could help them, if she wanted to. Or she could easily have them killed. They'd just have to get on her good side. "Back to the safe house?" he said.

"Back to the safe house," she agreed. "I know you're tired. Think you can handle driving the speeder back to the Bottoms?"

"Always."

CHAPTER 13

Qi'ra loved the freighter boneyard at night—the croaking bilgefrogs and creaking metal, the slap of wings on water, the pale moonlight against rusting hulks, the briny smell of fresh water meeting salt as the land sloped toward the ocean that she knew lay just over the horizon. More than anything, she loved the huge, ugly tree clinging stubbornly to her hill, and the way its roots had a strangling grip on the skeleton of her freighter. That tree was a survivor.

Her tree, her hill, her freighter skeleton.

This time, as they drove up to it in their stolen speeder, she was glad to have company. To share this place with . . . well, she wasn't ready to say they were *friends*, exactly, but Han and Tsuulo were okay to have around in a pinch.

"We're going to have a frost tonight," Han said as he parked the speeder. He blew on his hands as they all hurried inside her safe house. Qi'ra lit the lamp, noticing that the power was low. It would need a recharge soon.

They huddled around the lamp at the table. Qi'ra pulled out the holoprojector and set it before them.

She was about to thumb it on when she noticed Tsuulo shivering violently.

"You okay there, pal?" Han said.

Tsuulo blurted something, but Qi'ra only caught the word for "cold."

She grabbed the blanket from her cot and whipped it around his shoulders. "I wish we had more food," she said.

"I always wish I had more food," Han grumbled.

"It's hard to keep warm when your body isn't getting any energy," she said, and then she wondered if she'd given too much away, approached her secrets a little too closely.

Tsuulo chattered at them, and Qi'ra didn't have to understand Huttese to know that his words were jumbling together. Something was wrong.

"He's sorry to be a bother," Han said. "But Rodians don't do so well with the cold apparently? Something about the Rodian homeworld being hot, I dunno, he's not making much sense."

"I have a space heater," Qi'ra said, rummaging on the top shelf. "It's small, and it doesn't hold a charge long, but it might warm us up for an hour or two. Enough to keep him from going into hypothermia."

She found the heater, placed it on the table in front of Tsuulo, and flicked it on. It glowed against Tsuulo's face, turning his skin almost yellow. He sighed happily.

Between the lamp and the space heater, the safe house was as bright as it had ever been. For the first time, she noticed the skin of Han's face. It was bright red, as if he'd been standing in the sun for hours—all except for huge circles of white around his eyes where his goggles had been.

"What are you staring at?" he said.

"Your face," she said. "It looks burned."

"Oh, that. Yeah, it feels like it's going to crack. I got too close to the slag outtake."

"It's going to peel off in a day or two," Qi'ra said. "Unless we can find some bacta cream."

"At least I'll be harder to recognize with my face peeling away."

"Good point," she said, reaching for the holoprojector.

"Wait, what's that?" Han said, pointing to her right hand.

She saw her fingers through his eyes. They were bruised and swollen, especially the second knuckle of her middle finger. It throbbed something awful, but she didn't think it was broken. Besides, she'd had worse.

Qi'ra shrugged. "From when I punched Reezo. I told you it hurt." Next time she wanted to hit someone she'd remember to use a wrench or something instead.

Tsuulo jabbered at them, pointing to the holoprojector.

"Okay, okay, here we go," Qi'ra said, thumbing it on.

A figure popped up from the projector, limned in blue, barely taller than Qi'ra's table lamp. A female biped. She was too tiny, and the holoprojector didn't give them enough detail, to identify her species with certainty. Which was probably by design, Qi'ra figured. All they could tell was that she was slender, with long sweeping robes and a heavy cowl that completely covered her features. Her hands were clasped in front of her, and she bowed slightly, inclining her head just so.

"Greetings," she said.

"Greetings," Qi'ra replied. Her heart was in her throat. She was talking to an Imperial defector. Someone who was in the starry sky somewhere above them. It made her head swim.

"I expected this first attempt at an auction to have complications," she said. "I even expected to have to sacrifice some assets. But I did not expect my datacube to end up in the hands of three young scoundrels."

"Scoundrels?" Han said, appearing affronted, though Qi'ra had a funny feeling he was pleased.

"You went to a lot of trouble and risk to contact us," Qi'ra pointed out.

The figure in blue waved a dismissive hand. "I've had eyes on the ground the whole time, of course. And a tracker in that cube. That's another thing I didn't expect: for my cube to end up in Corellia's infamous freighter boneyard. Where starships go to die."

Tsuulo drew in breath. Han and Qi'ra exchanged an alarmed glance. The Engineer knew exactly where they were.

Then why wasn't she sending her pet stormtroopers after them? Why wasn't she taking the datacube back by force?

Qi'ra had the answer almost as soon as her mind formed the question: because it was unique. She had *defected* from the Empire. That meant she couldn't leave copies behind. The datacube contained her life's work, and she was worried they might destroy it.

It's why the stormtroopers at the Foundry had missed with their blasters. They didn't want to damage the cube.

"If you come after us," Qi'ra said, "we'll smash the cube to smithereens."

The figure nodded, "I've no doubt."

"But we don't want to do that," Qi'ra added hastily. "We'd rather agree to a better arrangement."

"I'm glad to hear it," the Engineer said. Her voice was low and husky, but it had a mechanical quality. Qi'ra didn't know enough about holoprojectors to tell if it was merely a function of long-distance communication or if the Engineer was altering her voice on purpose.

Qi'ra wasn't sure what to say next, and she was a little irritated, a little relieved when Han jumped in with, "So . . . should we meet up or something?"

"What for?" the Engineer said carefully.

She was being cautious, Qi'ra realized. She wasn't as poised and confident as she appeared.

Qi'ra smiled. "We want to give the cube back to you. But only you. Not an emissary. We've been running for our lives, you see, and I'm sure you understand how difficult trust can be in these situations."

Han was giving her a strange look. "You're really good at this," he whispered.

"I would love to see my cube again," the Engineer said. "I'd be happy to provide escort for you to my ship."

"You would?" Qi'ra said. "I mean, that's good."

"On one condition," said the Engineer.

"There's always a catch," Han mumbled.

"You must do something for me, first. To prove you're legitimate. A tiny favor."

Tsuulo let his head fall to the table in despair. Even Han slumped over, saying, "A *tiny* favor? Yeah, I bet."

Qi'ra wanted to scream with frustration. They'd been through so much already. What more did she want? But another part of her acknowledged the Engineer's sound strategy. In her place, Qi'ra would require a loyalty test too. Or at least a competency test.

Qi'ra felt weariness in her very bones. "Just tell us what you want," she ordered.

"The Empire tracked me here to the Corellia system," the Engineer explained. "I sent one of my crew members planetside to gather supplies, and CorSec recognized him and arrested him. He's being kept in a holding cell in downtown Coronet City."

Tsuulo swore, and even though his voice was muffled by the blanket, the sound must have carried, because the Engineer said, "Your Rodian friend is . . . colorful."

"You want us to retrieve your crew member?" Han guessed.

"I do."

"How?" Qi'ra said. "You can't just walk into a holding area and grab a prisoner."

"I'll provide uniforms and identichips that will get you through the door," she said. "The rest will be up to you. You three have proven very resourceful so far. I think your chances of success are . . . acceptable."

That didn't sound good at all. "What about your stormtrooper friends?" Qi'ra said. "They seemed pretty loyal to you."

The Engineer's chest rose and fell with a deep, controlling breath. "I'm sure a smart girl like you understands how imperative it is to use one's assets strategically and with circumspection."

Qi'ra's eyes narrowed as she puzzled that one out. "You . . . can't risk using them too often?" she guessed.

"Exactly. They veered off patrol once already today. Several of them discharged their blasters. It will be weeks, maybe months, before I can use them again without risking their posts. And I need them to stay right where they are, safe and above suspicion."

Han crossed his arms over his chest and frowned. "This seems like a very bad idea."

"If you do this for me," the Engineer said, "I'll arrange passage to my ship, get all three of you safely offworld."

Han sat up a little straighter, his eyes wide.

"How will you deliver uniforms and identichips?" Qi'ra asked.

"I'll give you the coordinates for a drop location. It will be someplace out of the way. I'll throw in a little surprise."

"I hate surprises," Qi'ra said.

"You'll like this one. It's something I cooked up in the lab. Should come in handy."

Qi'ra looked to Han and Tsuulo. "What do you think?" she said.

Tsuulo nodded, saying something that sounded affirmative.

"It's our best shot," Han said. "I've been in lockup a few times myself. I know my way around the place."

"Then we're agreed," Qi'ra said. "Give us the coordinates of the drop point, and all the information you can about the holding area, and we'll get your crew member back."

"I dare not risk using the holonet," she said. "So everything you need will be left at the drop point." She rattled off a set of coordinates, which Tsuulo typed into his datapad.

That meant they'd have to retrieve the Engineer's resources and *then* make a plan. Qi'ra would just have to work with that. "We have a deal," she said.

The Engineer inclined her head in acknowledgment, and the hologram winked out.

The three of them were silent a long moment. The lamp on the table sputtered. Not much time left before it went out completely.

"Well, that was interesting," Han said.

"I guess," said Qi'ra.

"You can come up with a plan, right?" he said. "No problem."

"Sure," she said weakly. "No problem." The truth was she was exhausted and hungry and totally out of her league. A weight pressed on her shoulders, crushing her down, making her feel small and helpless. She hated that feeling.

"You knew exactly what to say to her," Han marveled. "You're a natural at . . . well, not at talking to people in general. You're too stuck-up and detached for that."

"It's a wonder you don't have more friends, as encouraging as you are."

"What I mean is you're really good at the business side of things. And you sound like all those"—he waved a hand in a vague gesture—"important people. You're a player, Qi'ra, just like them."

"Thanks? I think?" But a little of that weight lifted, making her feel as though she could breathe.

Tsuulo said something about sleep.

"Yeah, maybe a couple of hours?" Han suggested.

The little Rodian hunched under his blanket, his bad antenna nearly flat against his head as he studied the coordinates on his datapad. He had to be just as exhausted as they were, maybe more so, given his difficulty with cold temperatures. Poor guy. She and Han had dragged him into this mess, and he had never once complained.

"Tsuulo," Qi'ra said. "You don't have to do this."

"Yeah, none of this is your fault," Han agreed.

He looked up at them, blinking his huge black eyes in confusion.

"I mean, if you just want to stay here," Qi'ra said,

"while Han and I get the Engineer's crew member, that's fine. We shouldn't have forced you to be part of all this, and . . . well, I'm sorry."

Tsuulo responded with rapid-fire words, and Qi'ra was pretty sure she'd made him angry.

"He says *of course* he's coming along," Han translated. "He's in it for the long haul now. Besides, you and I are . . ." Han's voice trailed off.

"What? What did he say?" Qi'ra demanded.

Tsuulo gestured at Han to keep translating.

"He says you and I are his friends. And Tsuulo never turns his back on his friends."

"Oh," Qi'ra said. She could feel her face, her heart, her soul freezing solid. Tight. Impenetrable . . .

Then Tsuulo smiled, that ridiculous Rodian grin that could only ever reach about the width of three human fingers, and Qi'ra realized with a thud in her chest that she *liked* the little fellow. She enjoyed his company. These past couple of days would have been unbearable without him. And without Han.

She cleared her throat. Han avoided their gazes, looking as uncomfortable as she felt.

"Well, Tsuulo," she said at last. "I can see why you and *I* are friends, but I have no idea why you'd want to be friends with *that* guy." She thumbed in Han's direction.

"Hey!" Han said, though he was smiling.

Tsuulo laughed, then he said something else that made Han frown.

"What?" Qi'ra prompted.

"He says everything will be fine. The Force is with him."

"Huh. I guess I'll take first watch," Qi'ra said.

"Wake me in an hour?" Han said, already heading toward the cot.

After everyone had napped they jumped into the speeder, and Tsuulo directed them to the coordinates of the Engineer's drop location. They skimmed across the freighter boneyard to the edge of the swamp, where the freshwater bog gave way to salt marsh. Muddy estuaries swirled through windblown grass, appearing as silver ribbons in the moonlight. Night fishers soared overhead, occasionally diving into the water. Scavenge droids on long stilts waded through the water looking for salvage and recyclables.

The three of them crested a small rise, and suddenly the sea stretched before them, a vast black expanse frothing with white. Tsuulo directed Han to stop.

A few meters more, and they'd meet the cold sand

and rock of Coronet's harsh shoreline. To their left a wide creek emptied into the ocean, the surface oily with darkness and . . . something else?

The wind blew into their faces, and Qi'ra nearly choked.

"What is that horrible smell?" Han said.

Qi'ra drew the lapel of her jacket over her mouth, but it did little good. The air was thick with sweet rot and sour garbage and something far, far worse. It was so strong it made her eyes sting.

Tsuulo said something that made Han gasp.

"He says it's sewage!" Han told her. "But that's not right. We practically live in the sewers, and it never smells this bad."

"Actually, I think it might," Qi'ra said. "We've been topside for more than a day. Our noses have readjusted."

Han gaped at her. "You mean the White Worm lair smells like this all the time? That means *we* probably smell like this all the time."

"You know what they say: 'You can smell a White Worm coming a klick away.'" It made her wonder how much perfume had originally been on the clothes that Lady Proxima left for her.

"Well, let's grab the Engineer's package and get out of here quick."

Tsuulo led them to small mound of rocks and sand and gravel, piled up like a cairn. The speeder headlamps lit the space as the three of them set to work clearing it away, and Qi'ra found herself moving too slowly, the weight of her thoughts making her sluggish.

The truth was, she didn't want to stink like a latrine. She didn't want to be dirty all the time. She didn't want to crash back into the dark sewers when she'd had a taste of open air and fancy clothes and beautiful hotels and the attention of powerful people who believed she had something to say.

"There!" Han said. "A cargo crate."

They opened it. True to the Engineer's word, the crate contained three neatly folded uniforms, counterfeit identichips, and a handful of credits.

"I don't see the one thing I was really looking for," Han said.

"What's that?" Qi'ra asked.

"A portable shower!"

She wrinkled her nose in sympathy. "There's a spot back that way with fresh water."

Han regarded her skeptically.

"Well, fresh-*er* water at any rate. We can clean up there a bit."

Tsuulo pulled two small round items from the crate.

Qi'ra didn't recognize them. He held one up and twittered a question. It fit in the palm of his hand like a children's toy ball, but its metal casing glittered in the light of the speeder's headlamps.

"I don't know," Han said. "There's a button right there; what does it do?"

Tsuulo was about to press it but Qi'ra yelled, "No!"

He froze.

"The Engineer said she was leaving a surprise for us," she explained. "What if it's a weapon of some kind?"

Han moved closer and peered at the thing in Tsuulo's hand. "Maybe it's a thermal detonator. I've heard about those."

Tsuulo handed it to Han, who turned it over, studying it from all angles. Meanwhile, Tsuulo retrieved his datapad and began sifting through information.

He made a noise of discovery and held up the pad for Han and Qi'ra to see. It displayed an image of something similar—small, round, and metal with a button on one side. It was labeled "stun grenade."

"This will come in handy," Han said with a grin. Then his grin slowly disappeared, as though he were realizing something unpleasant. "She probably gave us two in case we stunned ourselves by pressing the button on the first one."

"I think the Engineer designed these herself," Qi'ra said. "It's probably not your everyday stun grenade."

"There's an everyday kind?" Han said, and Qi'ra shrugged.

Tsuulo pulled a uniform from the crate and flipped it out. It was made of stiff, light gray material, with a high collar and a matching small-brimmed hat. Then Tsuulo swore, loudly and at length.

"Uh, Qi'ra? We have a problem," Han said. "These uniforms say 'Sienar Advanced Projects Laboratory.'"

"Blast," Qi'ra said, immediately beginning to revise all the plans she'd been considering. She'd heard the name Sienar plenty of times. But "Advanced Projects Laboratory" was new. "I'm not sure that company exists on Corellia," she said.

"Some kind of engineering corporation, right?" Han said.

"Maybe?" The three of them could never pass as scientists. They were way too young.

Tsuulo waved his datapad at them, chittering in Huttese.

"Oh, hell," Han said.

"What? What is it?" Qi'ra demanded.

"Tsuulo just plugged in our destination coordinates from the Engineer. Her crew member isn't sitting in a drunk tank or any regular lockup," Han said. "He's in an Imperial holding cell."

Qi'ra's breath caught. "You were right, Han, this 'favor' for the Engineer definitely has a catch."

"Some catch."

"Then we'll have to get creative, won't we?" she said. "Wait . . . what's that?"

Tsuulo had pulled three metallic items from the bottom of the crate. They were tube-shaped, with two protrusions along one side and a tiny grate along the other. They were small enough to stash in a pocket.

"Those are breathers," Han said. "I'm sure of it."

Qi'ra stared. "Why would we need . . . Oh." She looked from the breathers to the stun grenades and back again. "Those aren't stun grenades," she said, smiling. A plan was definitely forming. "They're something better."

CHAPTER 14

Han's face hurt like blazes. More than anything, he just wanted to let clean, cold water run over it. The pain from the burn was more serious than he'd let on, and it likely looked even worse. He'd be sure to attract attention. Then again, he'd seen a few aliens with red skin; maybe people would believe he was not quite human.

He was eager to change into the stolen uniform. His current clothes were filthy, damp, and cold. They'd scrubbed up at the place Qi'ra recommended, but there was only so much they could do without dumping their old clothes.

Despite that, Qi'ra was resolute about not putting on the uniforms until they were near the holding facility. "We shouldn't be seen wearing fancy lab uniforms while riding in this . . . thing," she said, indicating the speeder. "It would look suspicious."

She was right, so Han concentrated on piloting while Tsuulo and Qi'ra pored over a map of the holding area on his datapad. Qi'ra had sketched out a plan for them, and Han thought it just might work. It seemed simple and elegant to Han. All they had to do was lie really, really well. Easy, right?

The typical gloomy Corellian sky was back in force, but morning light cracked the horizon, painting the polluted clouds fuchsia and sapphire. Bilious exhaust rose from smokestacks in black silhouette against the sunshine. Lights from rusty boats glinted off the waterways as fishmongers brought their early morning hauls to the fish markets.

They crossed a bridge into central Coronet, and Qi'ra directed Han to an underground public parking facility, which would cost them a few of the precious credits the Engineer had given them. They stowed the speeder and changed into their uniforms under cover of darkness, each giving the others privacy.

Qi'ra patted her uniform down, adjusted the collar, and said, "So, do I look like someone who does business with Imperials?"

"Well, you certainly look imperious," Han said, and she rolled her eyes at him. The truth was she looked amazing. Sophisticated and strong. Like she was meant to wear such things.

Han looked away before his thoughts could betray him. "Do we walk from here?"

Tsuulo pointed toward one of the exits. "The address is One CorSec Plaza. It's not far. According to my map, a pedestrian walkway will take us from the parking structure to Peace and Security Headquarters."

"All we have to do is figure out which part of the building houses the Imperial holding block," Qi'ra said. "Then we walk right in."

She sounded like she didn't have a worry in the world, but Han knew her a little better now. When Qi'ra threw her head back like that, lifted her chin, and looked down on everyone else, it meant she was nervous.

With luck, no one else here would know her as well as he did.

Despite his own jitters, no one paid them any mind as they exited the parking structure and walked along the pedestrian path. Police speeders passed them, returning to headquarters after a long shift. A few stormtroopers flew by on speeder bikes, cutting in and out of traffic as though they owned the thoroughfare.

They reached an imposing white building fronted by vast marble steps. Thick columns rose on either side of the entrance, some kind of architectural homage to a distant history. Even though it was early morning, the area was heavy with foot traffic, mostly humans but a few other species as well.

As they mounted the steps, Han reminded himself that the entry and lobby area of Peace and Security Headquarters was public property. Anyone could go inside. All they had to do was blend in with everyone else, keep from being recognized.

A swaggering Sullustan pilot bumped into Han as he passed. Fighting his first instinct to turn and, well, *fight*, Han looked away quickly and pulled the brim of his hat lower to cover his face.

"I'm not sure wearing your hat so low is regulation," Qi'ra whispered.

"Regulations are stupid . . ." Han began.

But the words died on his lips, and Qi'ra and Tsuulo hastily ducked their heads and pulled down the brims of their own hats to cover their faces.

Because standing just outside the lobby was a Grindalid in an envirosuit. Han couldn't tell if he was one of Lady Proxima's soldiers or not, but he was clearly waiting there, watching for *somebody*.

Luckily, a uniform worked like a stealth cloak. The Grindalid glanced at them, and then his gaze slipped away like water. Han breathed a sigh of relief.

But he was on even higher alert now. The White Worms were still after them. The Kaldana Syndicate wouldn't let them die quickly. And if the Imperial stormtroopers saw through their disguises . . . Hadn't he heard somewhere that using false identichips was punishable by death?

They entered through doors that were large enough

to allow a commuter shuttle to pass. Han tried not to gawk at the atrium inside. The slick floors shimmered with marble or quartz or some material Han wasn't familiar with. The ceiling was lofty, at least four stories high, and hung with sleek, minimalist chandeliers that lit the space in bright white.

Ahead was a help desk, manned by one human and two droids. Beside it was a waiting area with several benches, many of them already occupied. To their left was a bank of turbolifts.

Qi'ra was looking around, calculating. She studied the benches, the desk, the walls, even the potted plants. Her gaze lingered on the two sentry droids standing guard near the lifts, then drifted to the security personnel patrolling the lobby perimeter.

"Your plan is going to work," Han assured her.

He really *hoped* her plan was going to work.

"Yeah, once we find the right cellblock. I'm looking for a posted map of the building. Government facilities are supposed to post floor plans, right? It's regulation. To show emergency exits. I thought it might tell us which part of the building was occupied by Imperials."

He and Tsuulo took up the search, scanning walls, looking for kiosks. All Han saw was an abstract painting that *might* have been a Corellian freighter zooming through space, and a larger-than-life portrait of Emperor

Palpatine. "I got nothing," Han said. "Just some creepy guy in a painting who seems to be looking at me no matter where I stand."

"I don't see anything either," said Tsuulo. "The great philosopher Flayshil Crena once said, 'That which you seek hardest to find remains hidden the longest.'"

"What does that even mean?" Han said.

Tsuulo shrugged. "Actually, I have no idea."

"This is no problem," Qi'ra said firmly, as if to herself. "No problem at all. We'll head toward the lifts. Maybe it's posted there."

"I think the lifts are for official personnel only," Han pointed out.

"We *are* official personnel, remember?" she said. "Besides, do you have a better idea?"

"As a matter of fact, I do," Han said. "Watch and learn." And with that, he strode forward to the help desk, Qi'ra and Tsuulo at his heels.

A woman was ahead of him in line. She pleaded with the droid clerk that her identichip had been confiscated by CorSec in error, that she couldn't afford to pay the speeder ticket fines, much less have her citizenship reinstated. A moment later, she fled in frustration, tears streaming down her face.

"May I help you?" asked a bored, mechanical voice.

"I certainly hope so," Han said, giving his best approximation of Qi'ra's imperiousness. "My"—he almost said *friends*—"colleagues and I are fresh off the shuttle from . . . er . . . Selonia, and we're late for an Imperial meeting. Please direct us to the right floor?"

"I didn't know Sienar APL scientists had interests on Selonia," the droid observed.

Han shrugged. "The Advanced Projects Laboratory has interests everywhere. And I don't question my orders. I just go where they tell me."

"That is wise," said the droid. "Please insert your identichip into the reader there." He indicated a slot mechanism that jutted from the table. "Once it checks out, I can clear you the whole way."

Han fumbled with the identichip inside his breast pocket, almost dropping it as he pulled it out. He shoved it into the reader, thinking *Please work, please work, please work*.

The reader whirred for a moment, then the indicator light turned soft blue.

"Everything checks out," the droid said. "The turbolifts are that way. Imperial offices are on the fifth floor."

"And the holding cells?" Han prompted.

"Why do you need to go there?"

"I'm afraid that's above your pay grade," Han replied.

"Fine. The holding cells are on the sixth floor. Have a nice day. If you are contacted with a survey, please indicate that I was helpful to you and that you left satisfied with CorSec's service."

Wordlessly, Qi'ra and Tsuulo inserted their identichips and were cleared to follow Han. The three of them headed for the lifts.

Qi'ra whispered, "Han, that was very well done."

He smiled so wide it made the burn on his face sting.

They entered the lift and punched the sixth floor. They had the capsule to themselves, so Qi'ra said, "Remember, don't detonate the ball thingies until I say. Getting in will be easy; we need them for getting out."

"Yes, ma'am," Han said with a mock salute.

The door of the lift slid open, and they stepped into a low-ceilinged vestibule filled with stormtroopers, even a handful of gray-uniformed officers. Han had to remind himself to breathe.

Okay, maybe not *filled*, exactly. Han counted five stormtroopers and two officers. If things went badly, it was seven against two. Seven blasters against two ball thingies, that is. Not the worst odds he'd faced.

"Tsuulo, pull out that datapad," Qi'ra whispered. "Try to look official."

Beyond the stormtroopers, a glittering shield blocked off a long hallway lined with cell doors on either side.

The Engineer's crew member was somewhere inside.

"Delightful," said one of the officers. "More lab grunts." He sat at a desk looking irritated. Han prepared for trouble. There was no one in the galaxy touchier than an Imperial officer stuck at a desk job.

"Lab grunts?" Qi'ra said, one eyebrow raised in a look of utter contempt.

This was the part Qi'ra had all planned out, so Han kept quiet, letting her take over.

The officer shrugged. "It's just what we call them," he said. He turned toward his console. "Looks like we're not expecting anyone. How can I help you?"

"We're here for Prisoner Two-Four-Eight-C," Qi'ra said. "He'll be coming with us."

"Is he being transferred?"

"Of course not."

"Then why—"

"He's needed for scientific inquiry." Word on the street was that the Empire had a business arrangement with certain favored corporate entities to provide subjects for weapons and environment testing. Sentient beings disappeared from the Imperial holding block all the time, especially nonhumans. Qi'ra was certain that was why the Engineer had provided these specific uniforms. Han hoped she was right.

The officer frowned. "You lab grunts with your

aliens. It's disturbing, I don't mind saying. Go ahead and scan your identichips, and I'll lower the shield."

They did as asked, and once again the reader indicator turned soft blue. The identichips were perfect counterfeits. Something remarkable had been encoded on them. Something that identified them as scientists with enough clout that even Imperial officers let them pass.

Of course, if Han had learned one thing from working for Lady Proxima, half of getting away with anything was acting like you belonged exactly where you were. When in doubt, brazen it out.

The officer hit a switch on his console, and the soft buzz of the shield went silent. He waved them through. "Go along now. The prisoner you're looking for is in cell nineteen. Do you want some help? He's a big fellow."

Qi'ra smiled serenely. "We came prepared. We'll be fine. Thank you, though."

"Sure. If you change your mind, just holler."

The stormtroopers moved out of their way, and the three of them stepped into the hallway of the cellblock.

"We have to hurry," Qi'ra whispered, quickening her pace. "Let's get this done before he thinks to comm his superiors about an unexpected visit."

They didn't have far to go to reach cell nineteen. In fact, Han would have felt better if it had been farther down the hall, away from the vestibule and the storm-troopers.

Han stretched on his tiptoes and peered through the tiny window in the door. The cell was dirty, with a single crooked cot holding an empty meal tray. Something long and hairy lay on the floor against the wall, its back to the door. Han could see why it was on the floor; it was way too big for the cot.

"Han?" Qi'ra prodded. "Anything?"

"*Something* is in there," Han said. "Not sure what. I think it's asleep."

Tsuulo said, "Let's just get this over with." He reached forward and palmed the door open.

It slid wide with a *whoosh* of fetid air; the cell hadn't been cleaned in who knew how long. The creature against the wall stirred, turned over—it was a Wookiee, Han could see now. As soon as the Wookiee saw them, he leaped to his feet with a roar.

"We're here on behalf of your boss!" Qi'ra said, talking fast and low. "The Engineer. She sent us to rescue you."

The Wookiee stopped mid-leap, landed easily, and cocked his head at her. He was a giant, at least two heads taller than Han, and his brown fur was streaked with white. Blue beads were woven into the hair flowing from his face, and his nose twitched incessantly, as though he was sniffing them.

Han knew a little about Wookiees; he'd encountered some while running errands for Lady Proxima, had even picked up a few words of Shyriiwook. But not enough to be useful. If this fellow didn't understand Basic, they were screwed.

"I have a plan to get you out of here," Qi'ra continued.

The Wookiee tossed his head, making a noise that was something between a groan and a yawn.

Han recognized one word. "He said 'food'!" Han told them. "Maybe he's hungry. Sorry, pal, I don't have any food, but we can take you to get some."

The Wookiee groaned again.

"'Ship'?" Han asked him. "Did you just say 'ship'?"

The Wookiee nodded vigorously.

"You're joking," Qi'ra said. "He made the exact same groaning sound as the last time."

Han blinked. "No, the sounds were totally different."

"Whatever," Qi'ra said. "Will you come with us?" she said to the Wookiee.

He shook his head violently.

"Blast. Why not?"

He growled something, but Han understood very little. "I think he doesn't trust us. Something about invisibility? No, disappearances! But I'm not sure."

Tsuulo said, "We don't have time to argue with him."

"We prepared for this contingency," Qi'ra said, reaching for her breather. Tsuulo and Han followed suit, and Tsuulo pulled the first "ball thingy" from his pocket.

The Wookiee roared.

"Now, Tsuulo!" Qi'ra shoved the breather against her nose and mouth.

The Rodian flicked the button on the stun charge.

The Wookiee leaped for Qi'ra, hands reaching for her throat.

The stun charge lifted into the air and spun, shooting yellow-green gas from tiny jets at its circumference.

The Wookiee faltered, then fell to one knee. His head lolled for a moment before he crashed to the ground.

"Dat dakes care of one probumm," Qi'ra said, her lips tight to the breather so no gas could enter her lungs. "Now we waid."

"How long will it dake?" Han asked. He knew they had to wait for the gas to dissipate for their plan to work, but if they took too long, those Imperials might get suspicious.

Tsuulo held up a hand as if telling him to have patience. After a moment, he lowered it and removed his breather. "Should be fine now. The gas disappears fast. I'm sure she engineered it specifically for stealth maneuvers."

Made sense. "Ready for the next step?" Han said to Qi'ra.

She nodded, taking a deep breath. Then she ran into the hallway, shouting, "Get in here at once! We have a huge problem, and I will not stand for it!"

Qi'ra could use some lessons in lying; she was overdoing it a bit. Nevertheless a flurry of boot steps indicated that people were coming their way fast.

The officer and two of the stormtroopers skidded to a stop just outside the cell.

"*Look* at this!" Qi'ra said, seemingly so angry she could breathe fire. "This prisoner is in terrible shape. What have you been feeding him? When I tell my superiors what you've done to our asset—"

"We did nothing!" the officer protested. "This isn't our fault! He was fine at the last feeding."

Qi'ra peered into his face. "You know a lot about Wookiees, then?"

"I . . . no, I guess not."

"Then how do you know he was fine?"

"I guess I didn't . . . I mean, his appetite was fine. He didn't give us any trouble."

Tsuulo pointed to his datapad and began jabbering at the Imperials, ostensibly instructing them on some basics of Wookiee physiology. In actuality he was insulting their mothers and wishing them bad bowels. Han kept a perfectly straight face. And hoped quietly that none of them understood a single word of Huttese.

Qi'ra tapped her bottom lip. "I concede that he may have already been ill when he was brought here. I suppose you can't be held responsible if he worsened in your care."

"Yes, that must be it! He was already ill when he was brought here."

"I may still be able to salvage him."

"Oh? How?"

"Can you have a med lift brought here? We'll push him out and get him to our ship. We have a well-provisioned infirmary."

"Absolutely. At once." The officer fled, the stormtroopers at his back.

"Wow, that actually worked," Han whispered.

Tsuulo started laughing quietly.

"What?" Han asked.

"The part about calling the Wookiee an 'asset' to be 'salvaged.' Qi'ra sounds just like a stuck-up Imperial."

Han translated for Qi'ra and was awarded with one of her magnificent smiles.

"You think this fellow is okay?" Han said, prodding the unconscious Wookiee with his foot.

"Should be," Qi'ra said. "I hope so. If he's not, this is all for nothing."

The officer returned, pushing a hovering gurney ahead of him. "Your med lift," he said.

"Perfect," Qi'ra said. "Your cooperation in this might mean the difference between life and death for my asset."

Again, Han felt she might be pushing it too hard, but the officer beamed. "Anything else?" he asked.

"Help us get him onto the lift?"

Together, Han, the officer, and the two stormtroopers lifted and heaved until the Wookiee lay across the gurney. His feet hung over the end, but Han figured it would hold.

"Thank you," Qi'ra said. "Now we must hurry."

She pushed the lift out the door and down the hallway. It glided through the air easily, as if the creature on it did not weigh more than Han, Qi'ra, and Tsuulo all put together.

"Han, get ready with the second ball thingy," Qi'ra said under her breath.

That meant she expected trouble. Han reached into his pocket for the gas bomb and palmed it, careful not to engage the button.

They reached the vestibule, where the other stormtroopers turned to gawk at the Wookiee on the gurney. They were almost to the lift. Just a few more steps . . .

"Hey, can I ask you a question?" the officer said at their backs.

Qi'ra ignored him, pressing the call button.

"How did a young, pretty girl like you get such an important job?"

Han felt his hackles go up. As if being pretty were somehow not compatible with being important. The Engineer's gas grenade was cool and hard in his hand, ready to be activated at a moment's notice.

"C'mon, tell me. How did you do it?"

Without turning around, Qi'ra said, "I did well in my aptitude testing."

"You're saying I didn't?"

Finally, Qi'ra turned, facing him down. "You're just an ensign, stuck in an office job on this dive of a planet. What do *you* think?"

A muscle in the officer's jaw moved. He reached for the comm. "You know, before you go, I need to check with my superiors. Make sure this is a sanctioned removal. I'm just an ensign, after all."

Softly, Qi'ra said, "Breathers. Now."

Han shoved his breather against his nose and mouth. Qi'ra and Tsuulo did the same.

"Hey, what are you—"

Han yanked the gas grenade from his pocket, flicked the switch, and tossed it into the air in one swift, smooth movement. The little metal ball spun in the air, spewing gas.

The lift opened.

"Go now!" Qi'ra said around her breather, pushing the gurney and its resident Wookiee into the lift. The sounds of choking and coughing peppered their backs.

The door slid closed behind them, and they began to descend. After a moment, Tsuulo removed his breather and shoved it into his pocket. The others followed suit.

"They'll be out a long time," Qi'ra said.

"I just hope he didn't open that comm before he lost consciousness," Han said.

"You sure the Wookiee is okay?" Tsuulo asked. "He got two doses of that stuff."

"I only understood the word for 'two.' . . . Blast!" Qi'ra said.

"Uh-oh, what?" Han prompted.

"Two doses! I didn't think of that. I should have." Her shoulders slumped. "Two doses of that gas might be fatal. I . . . I messed up."

Gently, Han put a hand on her shoulder. "I doubt it. He's a Wookiee. It would take a freighter full of that stuff to hurt him. And your plan was great. Simple and perfect." It was true. The best plans were simple. So elegant, so sneaky, that no one knew you were trouble until long after you were gone. He'd have to remember that. "Now we're just going to walk right out the front door."

And that's what they did. Prisoners being escorted

in and out was a common sight at CorSec headquarters, and few paid them any mind, even when it was a giant Wookiee on a med lift.

Moments later, they stepped into the cold Corellian day. No one had even sounded an alarm.

CHAPTER 15

Getting the Wookiee out of CorSec headquarters without drawing too much attention was one thing. Getting him through downtown Coronet to the parking structure was quite another.

As they traveled the pedestrian walkway with a giant furry creature on the med lift between them, Qi'ra was certain all eyes were on them. Was that Besalisk staring? That homeless beggar was probably a spy. And those lampposts—probably filled with hidden cams. If anyone decided to look for them right now, they'd be easy to find.

"Just walk casual," Qi'ra told them, mostly for her own benefit. "Eyes straight ahead as if we've nothing to hide."

They were almost to the parking structure when an alarm sounded, piercing the cold air, startling everyone around them. Instinctively, they all froze.

"No, no, we have to keep going," Qi'ra urged. "Pretend like nothing is wrong."

They kept going.

The siren wailed and wailed, loud and close. Too close. It certainly came from Peace and Security Headquarters. No doubt the officer's comm had gone through, just as Han feared, and when someone went up to investigate, they found a vestibule full of unconscious Imperials.

It would take CorSec and its resident Imperial officers a little time to gather their resources, interview witnesses, figure out who they were looking for. But not much time. The Empire had more resources than Qi'ra could imagine.

Resources. They were walking out of CorSec alive—with an Imperial prisoner, no less—thanks to the Engineer's resources. Everything was so much easier when you had money. Connections. Influence.

Someday, somehow, Qi'ra was going to have all of that.

She would have to do better, though. She was tired, sure. As hungry as she'd ever been. But she shouldn't have overlooked the possibility of the Wookiee inhaling a second dose of gas. And she shouldn't have let that ensign get under her skin. If she'd just left without saying anything, the alarm might not have been going off.

Most of all, she should have had a contingency plan for walking in and *not* finding a map posted. From now on she'd keep in mind that people didn't always follow regulations. It was a good thing Han was able to think on his feet. Come to think of it, they made a pretty good team. Qi'ra thought everything through, and when they met unexpected obstacles, Han improvised.

They entered the dark parking structure and found their speeder. The med lift was not quite level with the speeder, so the three of them had to heave the Wookiee up over the rear spoiler, rolling him into the back seat.

They crowded into the front seat, Qi'ra squashed between the two boys. Han guided the speeder out of the structure and onto the thoroughfare. She was glad for the excuse to put the riding goggles back on. They made her feel safer. Invisible.

It was a deceptive feeling, though, and she knew to be wary of complacency right now. The Wookiee was too big for the back seat; his hairy feet were sticking up over the side of the speeder. Of course they were going to be noticed.

All they had to do was get to the rendezvous point the Engineer had indicated. According to Tsuulo, they were headed toward some wealthy citizen's fancy estate at the edge of town, far enough away from the spaceport to not interfere with air traffic. Besides, no one would think twice about a small shuttle landing on one of the major estates. That kind of thing happened every day.

"Don't look now," Han said, "but I think that's a police speeder a few vehicles behind us."

Blast. Qi'ra forced herself not to look, but she and Tsuulo exchanged alarmed glances.

"Okay, I'm banking into a turn," Han said. "Look casually over your shoulder, as if taking in the sights, and tell me if that's a police speeder."

She did exactly as he asked, craning her head to stare at the buildings around them, sparing only a quick look for the speeders behind them.

Her heart thudded.

Sure enough, not far behind was a one-man vehicle with long stabilizers for easy maneuverability and a wicked-looking blaster mount.

"Definitely a police speeder," Qi'ra said. "It has a blaster turret."

Tsuulo said something about stormtroopers.

"Yeah, at least it's not one of them," Han said. "They're way better trained than CorSec officers."

Qi'ra risked another look behind them. The police speeder was gaining on them. "I think it's tailing us."

Han reacted instantly, taking a sharp turn onto another thoroughfare.

"So what do we do?" Qi'ra asked.

"I dunno . . . improvise, I guess. I've outrun CorSec before. I mean, I was on foot, in the sewers, but still."

"Uh, Han, that speeder turned where we did. It's definitely following us."

Tsuulo pointed to a nearby intersection, saying something about "home" or maybe it was "house."

"We can't, Tsuulo, not yet," Han said. "We have to get out of the center of town, *then* circle around and head for the outer estates."

"That speeder is not gaining on us," Qi'ra pointed out. "Why isn't it catching up?"

"That CorSec officer doesn't want to catch us," Han explained. "Their job is to keep us in sight and communicate our location to everyone else. Once enough speeders have been dispatched, they'll surround us. They might even dispatch a few waterspeeders, come at us from the canals."

"Holy moons." Qi'ra had no idea how they were going to get out of this one.

"That's why we have to get away from the downtown area. Okay, hold on tight. I'm about to do something stupid."

"Holy *moons*." She and Tsuulo grabbed the roll bar and held on for dear life.

They were approaching the seedy entertainment district. Cheap holoboards promised unspeakable delights while casting blue and red and purple motes onto their skin—even in the light of day. A portable projector sign was propped up outside a cantina, advertising the concert of some low-rent musician Qi'ra had never heard of.

"This is going to work," Han muttered. "It's going to work, it's going to work."

"You're about to hit that sign!" Qi'ra yelled.

"I know!" he yelled back.

Han hit the left reverse thruster, and their back end swept right, all the way around to the sign. Metal screamed as their rear fender sent the sign flying end over end into the street. Han reversed right and hit the accelerator, powering them back into the straightaway.

Everyone behind them swerved to avoid the sign, including the police speeder, which was forced to slow down to keep from crashing.

"You did that on purpose," Qi'ra said.

"I knew it would work!" His grin was so wide it took up the whole world. Han loved piloting, she realized. This was where he belonged.

Han took a quick turn. Then another.

They skimmed through town until the entertainment district and the fish markets were mere blips in their wake. Only then did Han steer them toward the neighborhood housing Coronet City's richest, most powerful residents.

"You think we lost them?" Qi'ra asked.

"Only temporarily. Once the stormtroopers figure out which prisoner we sprung and put it together that we're working with the Engineer, we're screwed."

Tsuulo asked Han a question.

"Don't even *think* that right now. If that happens, we're especially screwed."

"If what happens?"

"He's worried the Engineer won't be true to her word. That there won't be a shuttle waiting for us after all."

"There has to be!" Qi'ra protested. "We have her Wookiee!" She peered over her shoulder to check on him. He was still out cold, but he had shifted a bit. His right arm and most of his head were smashed into the footwell of the seat. She desperately hoped he was all right.

They sped through a neighborhood of tenements, tall buildings made of boxy apartments that were stacked haphazardly like children's blocks. Several barefoot kids played a game with a rope outside of one. Laundry hung from another. This area wasn't too different from the freighter boneyard, Qi'ra mused. People built whatever they could with whatever tools they had and called it home.

Soon the tenements ceded to a district dense with small, dingy factories, and finally to a wide, muddy river.

"Toll booth ahead," Qi'ra said.

"All toll booths are equipped with cams and recognition tech," Han pointed out. "Between that and the toll, they do a pretty good job keeping lowlifes like us away from all the fancy rich people who live across the river."

"So once we cross, they'll know we're here."

"Yep."

"Any other ideas?"

"Nope."

Tsuulo jabbered at them, waving his arms.

"You have an idea, Tsuulo?" Qi'ra asked.

"He has a terrific idea. He says that once we cross, we should go really, *really* fast."

Qi'ra slumped in her seat. They were definitely going to die.

They paused at the toll booth to insert their last credit chip. The barrier slid away, and they zoomed across the bridge into Coronet City's finest residential district.

The densely packed buildings and steaming pipe vents and endless paver that made up the rest of the city were not in evidence here. Instead, they cruised through quiet tree-lined streets bordering expansive lawns. Qi'ra had never seen so many trees in one place. Maybe they were specially imported. Estate homes were set back from the street, boasting picturesque fountains, walls of glass, and rooftop landing pads.

Tsuulo indicated that they should turn left, and Han complied. "Not far now!" Han shouted.

A whining sound made Qi'ra's neck tingle. She felt heat on her skin, turned, and looked up. A small starship was coming out of the sky, descending on them.

"Han, we've got company!"

He dared to glance back, then punched the console in frustration. "That's an Imperial patrol craft! There's no way I can outrun it."

"Two mounted cannons are pointed at us," Qi'ra said.

Tsuulo yelled something, and Han yelled back, "Good thinking, pal. Okay, hold on."

Han swerved from the thoroughfare and onto one of the lawns, aiming for a stand of trees. Turret fire clamored in their wake, slinging up chunks of sod.

"We're almost there," Han hollered.

Something growled, sending shivers up her back, and she turned again. It was the Wookiee, thrashing in his seat. He was waking up.

Han swept from side to side, wrenching Qi'ra's neck but making them a tougher target. Gunfire erupted all around them. A sickening *ping!-crunch* sounded. The back end of the speeder scooted sideways several meters, nearly sending them into a tailspin, but Han righted them and accelerated toward the trees.

"We've been hit," Qi'ra said, trying to assess the damage. The Wookiee groaned, but Qi'ra breathed relief when she didn't see an injury. The speeder was another matter. The right rear fender was a mess of warped metal. Dark liquid like syrup leaked from an exposed pipe. "I think we're leaking fuel."

They reached the copse of trees, and Han steered the speeder in and out of tree trunks as if he'd been doing it his whole life and not just a few days. The blast cannons went quiet. The lull was only temporary, Qi'ra knew. As soon as they were clear of foliage, it would start up all over again.

Tsuulo pointed to a structure ahead. The trees parted to reveal a large pool cabana, open on two sides, with a sparkling blue pool beyond. Han aimed right for it.

Fire erupted around them again. Han flew them straight into the cabana and out the other side. The ship dropped down, nearly on top of them.

Han plunged toward the pool, and they skimmed over the water. The air they displaced kicked up a huge wake, flooding the craft on their tail.

The patrol craft hung back to get its bearings, and Han sped for another copse of trees. "Almost there!" he said again.

Another estate opened up before them, even vaster

than the last, with rolling hills, an artificial lake, and a huge curving ramp that led to a landing pad high on the rooftop.

Tsuulo pointed, jabbering excitedly. They had arrived.

But there was no shuttle in sight.

Something heavy flopped onto Qi'ra's shoulder, making her jump in her seat and making Tsuulo squeal. It was the Wookiee, flailing awake.

"Hurry, Han!" she said.

"I don't see a shuttle!" he shouted. "Do you see a shuttle? It's supposed to meet us on that landing pad."

"Just the patrol craft, already catching up," Qi'ra said.

"Should I head up there?" Han asked. "Even though we don't see the shuttle?"

Qi'ra had no idea what to do. Police speeders and fake uniforms and starships and fancy estates were all so outside her range of experience. Maybe Han could give her just a little more time with his fancy piloting, and she could come up with a plan and . . . Oh, screw it.

"Han, I've got nothing. What do your instincts say?"

He grinned—that cocky, smug grin she was maybe starting to like a little—and said, "We should go for it. I'm feeling lucky!" And he aimed for the curving ramp that would take them to the top of the mansion.

The patrol craft was nearly on them again. Han sped

around and gained the top. The view from up here was beautiful; in any other circumstance, Qi'ra would have stopped to drink it in. Instead, she leaped from the speeder yelling, "Help me with this giant hairy thing!"

Han and Tsuulo jumped out and grabbed for the Wookiee, who flailed back at them. "Careful, he's waking up!" Han yelled.

The patrol craft swooped toward them. But behind, barely a mote on the horizon, was another craft.

"I think I see the shuttle," Qi'ra said. They managed to get a grip on the Wookiee and drag him to the ground. "Over here," she ordered, "behind the speeder. We'll take cover until the shuttle gets here." Which had better be soon. It would be no trouble at all for the patrol craft to readjust its position and come up behind them.

Something sharp assaulted her nose. Chemical fumes, all around them. Rising up from the growing puddle caused by the speeder's fuel leak.

Qi'ra realized she had made a terrible mistake.

"Back!" she screamed. "Get back! Away from the speeder. It might blow."

They hustled backward, the Wookiee's heels dragging on the ground. Qi'ra had no idea what kind of ordnance the patrol craft had been firing at them, but laser blasts would ignite that fuel easily.

They made it all the way to the edge of the landing pad. Now they had no cover, and there was nowhere to go.

The patrol craft hovered before them. A ramp dropped, and stormtroopers poured out, blasters in hand.

Tsuulo prayed, harder and faster than Qi'ra had heard yet.

The second craft, which had to be the Engineer's shuttle, zoomed out of the sky, swooping over the patrol ship, spinning one hundred eighty degrees to show them its rear, and touching down a hair's breadth from their huddled forms. Blaster fire thundered, but the shuttle took it all, protecting the three of them and their drugged Wookiee. The shuttle had a forward deflector shield, Qi'ra realized. A *really good* deflector shield.

A ramp dropped down, and a man with cropped black hair and narrow black eyes beckoned. "Hurry!" he said.

He didn't need to say it twice. The three of them lifted the Wookiee and stumbled up the ramp into a narrow cargo area. The ramp closed behind them.

The black-eyed man helped them lower the Wookiee into one of the jump seats and strap him in. "Buckle up," he ordered. "We're leaving hot."

Qi'ra had no idea what "leaving hot" meant, but she buckled up as fast as her fingers would allow.

The shuttle was small, built for only eight passengers—fewer if one of those passengers was a Wookiee. Ahead of them was a cockpit with two pilot seats, facing a large viewing window. Stormtroopers continued to fire at them. The patrol craft still hovered above the landing pad, and its cannon turrets were rotating to give the shuttle a direct hit.

Their bright-green speeder reflected sunlight and laser bolts as it lay bleeding on the landing pad. Qi'ra's chest twinged with something unfamiliar. It was as if she liked that speeder, as if she was sad to leave it behind.

A stray blast hit the speeder, tipping it violently. Seconds later, it erupted into a massive fireball, filling the viewing window with roiling flames.

Tsuulo let out a strange keening sound that made the hair on Qi'ra's arms stand straight up. His snout trembled for a moment, then he turned his head to the side, refusing to look at the smoking scrap heap that was his brother's speeder.

Then the shuttle's thrusters kicked in, so hard and fast that they overcame the acceleration compensators, and Qi'ra's rear pressed tight into her seat, the belt digging at her waist.

The estates fell away beneath them, growing smaller and smaller. The world widened to reveal all of Coronet City, with its industrial islands and muddy waterways, all cozied up to a vast ocean. Corellia itself became an immeasurable curved horizon, and then a vast bluish orb clothed in rusty clouds, and finally, a distant mote of white in an expanse of empty blackness.

CHAPTER 16

It was like a punch to Han's gut, watching Reezo's speeder blow to smithereens. But as their shuttle left the planet's atmosphere, regret gave way to breathtaking wonder.

Han was in space. He could hardly believe it.

He'd always thought it would be dark and black. Instead it was as bright as day, and he could see everything from the hull of the shuttle to Qi'ra's face to Corellia's nearest moon in bright relief and perfect detail.

The planet grew distant, becoming a tiny shining dot. Unlike the planet, the sun Corell didn't seem any smaller from here, just whiter. Maybe brighter.

Space, it turned out, was huge. A man could have a lot of room all to himself out here.

The shuttle drifted into a turn, aiming for the edge of the solar system. Han watched the pilot closely, watched how his hands danced over the controls—so many of them! Piloting a starship was completely different from piloting a speeder, apparently. You had to think in three dimensions. Even though the ship itself had artificial gravity, out in the black of space, there was nothing to tell you which way was "down."

The proximity sensor pinged.

"What was that?" Qi'ra said.

"We've got Imperials on our tail," said the pilot. "They followed us from Corellia."

The shuttle shook with an impact.

"They're firing on us!" Tsuulo said.

"Preparing to jump to hyperspace," said the copilot.

Han's heart was a drum in his chest. He was finally going to see hyperspace.

A second impact wrenched his neck. It would have thrown Han across the shuttle if not for the harness of his jump seat.

"In three," the pilot said, "two, one." He pulled back on a lever.

Han felt a lurch in his belly, as if he'd just fallen. His ears popped, and the stars suddenly stretched into bright lines of light.

He could hardly breathe. It was like they were traveling through a tunnel of light, and it was the most beautiful thing he'd ever seen in his life.

It was over in mere seconds. The ship dropped back into real space, and though the shuttle's compensators made the transition as smooth as Corellian brandy, he felt the change in his very bones.

The pilot twisted in his seat to check on his passengers. "Everyone all right back there?"

Actually, Han thought he might be sick.

"You're looking a little green, kid. First time in hyperspace?"

Han nodded, not trusting himself to open his mouth.

"You get used to it," the pilot assured him.

The Wookiee whined, something about "wet" or maybe "water."

"Didn't think we'd see you again, Roo," the pilot said to the Wookiee. "Glad to have you back. Though I have no idea what you're saying."

"I think he's thirsty," Han choked out through his nausea. He turned in his seat to find the Wookiee nodding vigorously.

"We're almost there," the pilot said.

"Thirst is probably a side effect of that gas," whispered Qi'ra. "At least he's not attacking us." Then her eyes narrowed. "What are you staring at?"

He was staring at *her,* and her chin-length brown hair, and her eyes that seemed to change color with her mood. He said, "It just occurred to me . . . we're alive! I mean, I really thought we were done for back there."

"We're not out of this yet," Tsuulo pointed out, just as Qi'ra said, "The Engineer will probably kill us as soon as she gets the datacube."

Han glared. "I'm surrounded by pessimists."

"Hey, isn't that the sun?" Qi'ra said, pointing. "I thought lightspeed would take us far away from Corellia."

"It was just a feint," the pilot explained. "To lose our pursuers. We're heading for that asteroid cluster. The Engineer's ship is hiding there."

"You can do that?" Han said. "Exit hyperspace close to where you entered?"

"Well," the pilot said, grinning, "not *everyone* can do it. And truth be told, we're not that close; we traveled all the way across the system. We still covered a distance that would have taken days to travel at sublight speed."

"So you're a *good* pilot," Han said.

"Kid, I'm one of the best."

The Wookiee growled.

"Not as good as Kirroo back there," the pilot amended hastily. "Roo might be the best pilot I've ever met. The Engineer is going to be really glad to get him back."

The asteroid cluster he'd pointed to seemed like a jumble of whitish-gray pebbles floating in space, but as they neared, Han revised his assessment. The asteroids were huge, easily able to hide a starship. If you could somehow mash them together, you'd end up with a small moon.

The shuttle veered close to one of them, so close that Han could see its porous surface, along with several impact craters. It was the largest, vaguely round, and the shuttle rumbled a little, compensating for the asteroid's light gravitational pull. The other asteroids nearby were irregular; one was even jagged, like a chunk of it had recently been sheared away.

"Tsuulo, you've been in space before, right?" Qi'ra said.

The Rodian nodded. "I was really young when we left Coruscant, but I still remember everything about that trip."

Han translated, and Qi'ra added, "Yeah, I'm not going to forget this as long as I live."

"Which might not be very long," Tsuulo added cheerfully.

The shuttle swung around the asteroid, and a starship appeared before them. Han and Qi'ra gasped.

It was shiny and sleek, with curved lines and a reflective hull—totally different from the messy, irregularly shaped Corellian ships he'd seen his whole life. Several levels of viewing decks shone with artificial light. Bright red glittered along the edges of glowing blue drive units. The red was an aesthetic choice, Han realized. Like Reezo's holo-flames attachment.

"That's . . . beautiful," Qi'ra breathed.

"That's the *Red Nimbus*, an AC-Seventy-Five-P yacht liner," the pilot said. "A luxury cruiser manufactured on Nubia."

Han had heard of yachts, pleasure barges with every possible amenity, used by the galaxy's richest citizens. He never dreamed he'd lay eyes on one like this, much less board it.

Though, looking at the *Red Nimbus* through the viewport, he couldn't help thinking that it wasn't for him. Those red lights, the shimmering hull, the overwrought name—it all spoke to form over function. His friend Bee at the garage would have hated it. Han himself would take a messy, jumbled, *fast* Corellian cruiser over a luxury yacht any day.

Qi'ra obviously didn't share his opinion, though. She stared at the massive yacht, mouth agape, her heart in her eyes.

The pilot aimed directly for the side of the yacht. A small docking port jutted out of it. The pilot's and copilot's hands flew over the console, making adjustments as the shuttle slowed, pivoted, and backed into the port. It was going to be a perfect fit, like an identichip clicking into a reader slot.

The shuttle lurched, and a hollow metal sound echoed through Han's chest. The docking clamps had engaged.

"You can unclasp your belts now," the pilot said.

The back of the shuttle opened; the ramp lowered and hit with a thud. Light nearly blinded them.

The Wookiee was out of his seat and down the ramp faster than Han could blink. Several figures in white uniforms waited for them, standing in a small cargo bay. The Wookiee rushed over to them and gave each one a massive hug. One young man in particular was lifted from his feet, and he grinned widely, patting the Wookiee on his hairy back. "Good to see you, Roo!" he said.

Han, Tsuulo, and Qi'ra followed the Wookiee more slowly, the pilot at their heels. "That's the servant staff," the pilot explained. His expression saddened. "We already lost two of our own, cut down by Kaldana during the auction. So we're very glad to have our friend back."

"What now?" Han asked. The cargo bay contained a small freight lift for hauling supplies. The lift rose to a second level with a glass-encased booth perfect for overseeing the cargo bay, and—Han was willing to bet—sealed well enough that the bay could be vented in a pinch.

"I have to run a maintenance check on my shuttle," the pilot said. "Standard procedure after taking fire. That's the Engineer's personal assistant there. He'll take you to see her."

"Thank you," Qi'ra said, reaching for his hand and shaking it. "For getting us off Corellia. You saved our lives."

"Yeah, thanks, pal," Han echoed. "We owe you one."

The personal assistant was a small, balding man with a very round belly that overhung the waist of his pants. "This way," he said. "My mistress is anxious to meet you all."

They followed him up the lift, through the glass booth, and past a galley busy with three chefs. Something smelled amazing—warm and meaty and gently spiced. Han's stomach growled in response.

"I'm so hungry," Tsuulo whispered. "It feels like my stomach is eating itself."

Han knew the feeling.

After the galley, they passed through a corridor with lush red carpeting, limned with red floor lights. Paintings hung on the walls at regular intervals. Maybe they were fine art, worth millions of credits each. If so, what a waste.

The corridor ended with a short stairway, which took them to an elegant viewing deck. A fully stocked bar stretched along one wall. Beside it was furniture for lounging—a divan, a long couch, several reclining swivel chairs—all oriented to take best advantage of the glorious view.

Because the entire opposite wall was a viewport that looked right into the heart of star-studded space. A whole wall. Made of space-worthy glass.

Han couldn't imagine how expensive that was. Or why it was even necessary. If this ship were his, he'd be spending all his time in the cockpit anyway. The only viewport he'd ever need was the one in there.

Standing before the giant viewport was a tall, slender woman. Her back was to them, and she wore a gauzy silver gown with a low back that exposed smooth dark skin. Her dense black hair gave her an extra half meter of height; it was wound high on the top of her head, held in place by a silver scarf, the end of which drifted down her long neck. She held a wine glass in her left hand.

"You have a plan for this part, right?" Han whispered to Qi'ra.

Qi'ra shook her head and mouthed *no.*

"Dear Force, please help," Tsuulo muttered. "Don't let this lady kill us."

The lady in question turned and stared at the three of them. After a moment, her lips turned up into a smile— as choreographed and careful a smile as Han had ever seen.

She was extraordinarily beautiful, with full lips set off by a strong jaw and wide brown eyes that turned up slightly at the corners. Dollops of white makeup were painted on her cheeks in the shape of teardrops, a sharp contrast to her dark skin. The only thing giving away the fact that she was not human was her nose; it lay nearly flat against her face, and her nostrils were slit-like, almost Grindalid in nature.

"Welcome aboard the *Red Nimbus*," she said in a low, breathy voice.

"Uh, thanks," Han said. *Uh, thanks*? That's all he had? What happened to Improvise Guy?

"Are you the Engineer?" Qi'ra asked.

"I am."

"In that case, thank you for the extraction," Qi'ra said. "And for bringing us aboard your ship. The *Red Nimbus* is beautiful."

The Engineer waved a dismissive hand. "It was the least I could do for the young scoundrels who kept my datacube out of enemy hands. Not to mention returned my Wookiee to me. I'm very glad to reacquire him; he's my most valuable asset."

Reacquire. Asset. The words didn't sit right in Han's gut.

Tsuulo jumped in with, "What should we call you?"

Han almost translated, but Qi'ra beat him to it. "I'm Qi'ra. These are my friends Han and Tsuulo. Tsuulo just inquired about your name."

Qi'ra was better at Huttese than she'd realized.

"I'm afraid I have to keep that to myself. For now, call me Jenra. It's a title from my homeworld, and I suppose it will serve as a name."

Qi'ra gave her a smile as careful and choreographed as Jenra's own. "It's a pleasure to meet you, Engineer Jenra."

Jenra studied Qi'ra for a moment, her head cocked as if evaluating the girl. Then she took a sip of wine and stepped toward them, her silver gown swishing at her ankles. "Do you have my cube?" she asked, extending her hand.

Han looked to Qi'ra and Tsuulo, who both nodded at him. So he reached into the pocket of his vest, fished it out, and placed it in her warm palm.

She looked close, her eyes plainly assessing it, then her fingers closed around it as her chest rose and fell with a deep breath. "Thank you," she said. "Now, forgive my bluntness, but you all look terrible. Like you've been running for days without sleep."

"I'm sure we smell even worse," Han grumbled.

Again, that careful smile. "I wasn't going to say. In any case, I invite you to enjoy the hospitality of my yacht. I can offer comfortable sleeping quarters, food, and drink." Her nostril slits flared. "Also, bathing. And my staff can launder your clothing."

Qi'ra sighed, probably louder than she meant to. "That sounds incredible."

"I'm going to assess the cube for damage," Jenra said. Han's alarm must have shown on his face, because she held up a placating hand. "You did your best, I know, but the cube has been through a lot, and I need to make sure the data is intact before we make a plan. In the meantime, my assistant will escort you to the head, where you can bathe and change, and then to your sleeping quarters. After you've had some rest, and if you're interested, he'll give you a tour of the yacht."

"Oh, I'm interested!" Han blurted before he could stop himself. "I'd really love . . ." Everyone was staring at him, so he brought it down a notch and said more carefully: "I'd like to see the cockpit, please."

"That can be arranged," Jenra said, and this time her smile was indulgent. "Eat, rest, and tour. And then we'll talk."

CHAPTER 17

Qi'ra was so tired she was barely aware of shucking off her clothing and stepping into the shower. Cleaning jets hit her skin at just the right temperature and pressure. The heat penetrated her muscles, relaxing her shoulders, making her legs feel like jelly. Too soon the jets turned off, replaced by dryers that whisked moisture away. Then a light mist of nutrient-rich oil covered her skin and hair; she was delighted to discover that she didn't feel sticky at all, just soft. Refreshed.

She stepped from the shower and found that her sewer-stained clothing and even her boots were gone, replaced by a simple white tunic, which she pulled over her head. It fell mid-shin, leaving her feet and ankles exposed. Qi'ra palmed the sliding door open and stepped out of the bathing cubicle.

Engineer Jenra's personal assistant was waiting outside, along with Han and Tsuulo, who were freshly clean and wearing white tunics of their own. She'd never seen Rodian feet before. Tsuulo's toes were a lot like his fingers—long, green, tipped by suction cups. She forced herself not to stare.

Han was grimacing, looking stiff and uncomfortable in his tunic. "We smell like *roses*," he said, as if it were the worst thing in the galaxy.

"Better than sewage," Qi'ra said.

Jenra's assistant guided them to a tiny bunk room with four beds—two against each wall.

Tsuulo immediately claimed a top bunk. Han fell into the one below his, and Qi'ra grabbed the bottom bunk across from him. The white linens were smooth, almost silky, and the pillow was as soft as a cloud. As she sunk into the mattress, it contoured itself around her, buzzing lightly with a relaxation frequency and the perfect amount of gentle warmth.

She tried to keep her eyes open. She had to think. They weren't safe yet, not really. Maybe she could convince the Engineer to . . .

Sleep stole her thoughts.

She woke to a hand shaking her shoulder. Qi'ra peeled her eyes open and discovered Han bending over her, the bright red of his burned face very near. Tsuulo was right behind him, peering over his shoulder.

"Qi'ra," Han said. "Jenra's chefs made food for us. Do you want to come? Or would you rather sleep?"

Food might be the only thing that could get her out of bed right now. Just the mere thought made her feel like there was a hole of aching emptiness where her belly ought to be.

"How long did we sleep?" she asked, rubbing her eyes and sitting up.

"Not sure."

Tsuulo opened up the chrono on his datapad and twittered something.

"He says we slept ten hours," Han translated.

"I guess we needed it." Qi'ra got to her feet, noticing that both Han and Tsuulo were back in their old clothes—still threadbare and dingy, but clean and fragrant.

"Uh, we'll step outside and give you some privacy," Han said. "Your clothes are folded there." He indicated the foot of her bed.

A moment later, she was alone in the bunk room. She tore off the white tunic and donned her leggings and skirt, her red top and beige jacket. The skirt's color was ruined. It was still sturdy, still functional, but the deep, pure black of its youth was gone, replaced by streaks of white and gray and a badly bleached hem. Someone had even sewn up the spot she had torn, although it didn't look quite right. Everything else was in decent shape. The top had turned out especially nice; whoever had laundered it managed to remove almost all the stains without fading the color. Maybe they'd injected a little dye. Whatever the case, Qi'ra was grateful.

The others were waiting outside. "Took you long enough," Han snapped.

Qi'ra stared at him. Han was impulsive and insensitive, but he was never purposely rude to her.

He seemed to realize it, because he suddenly appeared sheepish. "Sorry," he mumbled, running a hand through his hair. "It's just I'm so hungry I could eat a raw screerat."

"Ew," Qi'ra said, though she could sympathize.

She expected to be led to the galley. Instead Jenra's assistant escorted them back to the viewing lounge. The Engineer herself was stretched across the divan, ankles elegantly crossed as she sipped a glass of wine, but Qi'ra hardly noticed because the air was thick with the scents of butter pastries and meat pies, steamed vegetables and fruit cider, and a dozen things she couldn't identify because she had never, ever in her short life smelled so many types of food.

Her mouth filled with saliva, and she looked around, maybe a little too desperately. There. The bar. Platters were laid out along the metal counter.

"Help yourself," Jenra said, waving them toward it all.

As one, they raced forward. Han grabbed an entire meat pie in his hands and bit off a huge chunk. "Ow!" he said around a mouthful. "Sthill thoo hoth!" He kept chewing anyway.

Tsuulo grabbed a delicate fork and speared a long tube-shaped object. It was covered in some kind of gravy, and it wobbled on his fork. He slurped it down, then chattered happily at them.

"Gross," Han said. "Tsuulo says they're called dree-bees. A kind of slug. It's a Rodian delicacy."

In any other circumstance, Qi'ra would have found that disgusting, but she was busy slapping butter on to a fluffy warm biscuit. She shoved it in her mouth, letting the flavor coat her tongue. She could almost weep.

After gulping down the biscuit, she tipped the pitcher of ice-cold fruit cider to her lips and downed fully half of it without taking a breath.

"You know," the Engineer said in an amused voice, "I had the staff set out some fine dinnerware and utensils for you, but I guess that works too."

The three of them stopped mid-gulp to stare at each other. *We look like desperate sewer kids who've never had a decent meal in their lives,* Qi'ra thought. But then she shrugged it off and grabbed a poached egg dripping in cream sauce.

A few bites later, Qi'ra began to feel sick. She wasn't used to rich food. Or any food, really.

She set down the piece of cake she was eating and started to wipe her mouth with the back of her hand. Then she thought better of it, grabbed a cloth napkin instead, and dabbed daintily.

Qi'ra folded the napkin and set it down. When she looked up, she discovered the Engineer staring at her. "If you're finished eating," she said, "come and join me." She patted the lounge chair beside her.

Qi'ra obeyed. Han and Tsuulo paused eating long enough to watch her walk toward Jenra and settle herself in the chair.

"I think I might be sick," Han announced to no one in particular.

Tsuulo nodded enthusiastically, then noisily slurped down another dreebee slug.

Ugh. Qi'ra had definitely eaten too much, too fast. She wasn't feeling so good herself.

"So," she said, turning all her attention to the Engineer so as not to be reminded of food, especially dreebees. "Did the datacube check out?"

Jenra took a sip of wine and said, "There was a small amount of degradation, but I was able to recover it. We found a strange residue inside; during the course of your adventures, did the cube by chance become submerged in liquid?"

No sense denying it. "We swam through an underground cistern while being chased by White Worms."

"My technician suggested that the liquids were more like digestive enzymes. . . ."

Qi'ra smiled and tried very hard not to look at Tsuulo or Han, even when Tsuulo loudly slurped down another slug. "The water underground has a lot of contaminates," she offered.

"It sounds like you've had an interesting few days."

"If by interesting you mean terrifying."

"Tell me all about it."

Qi'ra pressed her mouth shut. She was so used to keeping secrets. Telling the Engineer what they'd been through went against years of habit. But she couldn't think of a good reason to keep anything from her. Qi'ra glanced over at Han and Tsuulo, still nibbling at the bar. Han shrugged as if to say, *Sure, tell her.*

So Qi'ra started at the beginning with the assignment from Lady Proxima, the Kaldana representative becoming violent when the Droid Gotra won the bid, the flight through the sewers with Han, and then with Han and Tsuulo.

Han wiped his mouth on his sleeve and jumped in to fill in details from his perspective: the meeting in the Foundry, the attack by the Kaldana, his own escape.

Qi'ra picked up the story again with their brief respite at her safe house—although she was careful not to describe it in too much detail. Tsuulo explained the part about stealing his brother Reezo's speeder, with Han translating, and then Qi'ra finished up with the fake race through the streets of Corellia and their conversation with a badly damaged droid named Tool.

"Then we had to escape from the Foundry," Qi'ra said.

"That's where this happened," Han said, pointing to his burned face.

Qi'ra said, "And where your pet stormtroopers gave us your holoprojector."

Tsuulo finished eating slugs and joined them, taking up the seat opposite Qi'ra.

"You're the boy with the datapad," Jenra said. "The one I gave coordinates to."

Tsuulo nodded.

"We wouldn't have made it here without Tsuulo," Qi'ra said.

"I think they wouldn't have made it here without *you*," Jenra said, leaning forward, gazing at Qi'ra intently.

The attention made her uncomfortable. "I guess."

"Tell me how you retrieved my Wookiee."

"That was easy," Qi'ra said. "We had resources, thanks to you."

"Still, you walked right in and out with him. How?"

Han said, "We brazened it out. Well, mostly Qi'ra. She's good at that."

The Engineer leaned back on her divan and tapped a finger to her lip, considering them. She wore a sparkling red gown this time, with sculpted shoulder pads that rose into vicious points above her head. Her shoes seemed made of glass, with a wedge heel that added a hand's span of height. Qi'ra couldn't imagine dressing that way. You never knew when you had to run for your life, much less get through a doorway.

"You've all proven remarkably resourceful," she said. "Especially you, Qi'ra."

Qi'ra narrowed her eyes, instantly suspicious. Han had saved them more than once with his intuition. Tsuulo had come through for them with his mechanical skills. She wasn't deserving of praise any more than they were. "I had good people with me," Qi'ra said. "We made a great team." And she meant every word.

"I suppose you're right," Jenra said.

"What about you?" Han asked. "How did you get away from the Empire?"

"Well, it took years of careful planning," she said. "Of cultivating assets. Keeping my head down and my ears open. I spent two decades sending money to an untraceable account on an Outer Rim planet. Small amounts, so I wouldn't attract attention."

Tsuulo blurted a question.

"He wants to know how old you are," Han said.

Jenra smiled. "Old enough to be your grandmother. My species is long-lived compared to humans. I was already an old woman by your accounting by the time I acquired my Wookiee and my ship."

Han looked away, frowning. Something about that last sentence had bothered him, though Qi'ra didn't know what.

She asked, "How did you end up with this incredible yacht? I guess the Empire pays well."

"The Empire does pay fairly well . . . but not *that* well."

"Then . . ." Qi'ra stopped herself. She'd once heard that rich people considered it gauche to discuss money. Which was totally impractical. It was the thing everyone needed most; why wouldn't you discuss it?

"I had to get creative," Jenra said.

Qi'ra had no idea what that meant, but Han said, "You mean by selling Imperial secrets, for instance?"

She smiled. "For instance."

So she'd been doing this sort of thing for a while.

"But there's no going back this time," Qi'ra observed. "This time, you're leaving the Empire, making a run for it."

"Yes."

Han's eyes were wide, his lips slightly parted. "You can go anywhere," he breathed. "With a ship like this"—he gazed out at the myriad stars—"the whole galaxy is at your fingertips."

Jenra sipped her wine. "Would you like to have your own ship someday?"

Han gave her a disgusted look. "How's somebody like me going to get his own ship?"

She shrugged. "You never know."

"Well, I have a speeder," Han said, almost defiantly. "I've been tinkering. It's not a starship, but . . . it's going to be great."

Jenra nodded, as though she were agreeing with him. "I guess there's nothing wrong with small ambitions."

Qi'ra couldn't stop herself from jumping to Han's defense. "Han is an incredible pilot. A decent mechanic too. He learns fast. And he already knows several languages. I can easily see him flying around the galaxy with his own ship someday."

Han stared at her. She stared back. There was a question in his eyes, but she couldn't tell what he was asking.

It made Qi'ra uncomfortable, so she blurted, "Jenra, I bet you've been from one end of the galaxy to the other. I bet you've seen everything."

Jenra swung her long legs over the edge of the divan

and sat up straight. She put her empty wine glass on the side table and placed her hands in her lap. Her fingernails were short, her fingertips thick with callouses, her bare forearms corded with muscle. Jenra was certainly elegant and rich, but she also worked hard. She'd probably been working hard for decades.

"I've seen a lot, yes. My employment with the Empire took me all over, to all sorts of worlds, investigating technology, trying to find applications for it. That's my title, by the way. Senior applications engineer. So, for instance, when we discovered a toxic mushroom on Drashima III, my staff figured out how to distill it into an anesthetic gas, and then I designed a delivery vehicle, weaponizing it."

"Those gas bomb thingies you gave us," Qi'ra said.

"Yes. My very own design."

"Have you been to Coruscant?" Han asked eagerly. "Tsuulo was born there."

"Lots of times."

Tsuulo sat forward in his seat, and his black eyes widened as he asked Jenra a question.

"He wants to know if you've met any Jet-eye," Han said. Then to Tsuulo, "What's a Jet-eye?"

"Jedi," Jenra corrected. "I've met a few. But they're all dead now."

Tsuulo sat back, slumping in his seat.

"Huh," said Han, eyeing the Rodian. "Whoever they are, I hope they put up a good fight."

"Not really," said Jenra.

There was only one thing Qi'ra wanted to know. Softly, tentatively, she asked, "What's it going to take?"

"What do you mean, my dear?" Jenra said.

"To feel safe. To survive. To be free of the people chasing you once and for all."

Jenra leaned forward. "Do *you* feel safe, Qi'ra?"

"Never."

"You have your answer. I'll try to sell the plans again, and once the deal goes through, I'll disappear— somewhere on the Outer Rim where even the Empire doesn't touch. I've been planning this a long time, and I have every confidence that things will go as I have foreseen. But I will never let myself feel safe."

Qi'ra noted the slight contradiction. *I have every confidence. . . . I will never feel safe. . . .* Maybe that was the trick. Be confident, but ever alert.

The next question on the tip of her tongue was, *Why are you being so nice to us? Why didn't you throw us out of the airlock as soon as you got your cube back?*

But the answer came to her, and she kept her mouth shut. Jenra was showing them hospitality because she still needed them. But why? Something that had to do with selling her shield generator plans . . .

"How has that been going?" Qi'ra asked, probing. "Selling the datacube, I mean?"

"Oh, fine," she said. "We will hopefully have another auction soon."

Hopefully, not definitely.

"The Empire's presence on Corellia has definitely grown since you arrived," Qi'ra pointed out.

Tsuulo made a noise of agreement.

"They tracked you here somehow. I wouldn't be surprised to learn that all the potential buyers are a little gun-shy," Qi'ra went on. "Or stalling while they figure out if it would be more beneficial to simply turn you in."

"I bet there's a huge price on your head," Han said. "More money than I can imagine."

Qi'ra gave him her best *Be careful!* look.

Han immediately put his hands up and said, "Not that we'd ever turn you in! We're just glad to get out of all this alive."

Jenra studied the three of them in turn, as if considering. After a moment, she said, "I admit, although there has been considerable interest in a second auction for the cube, buyers have been slow to come to the table."

Qi'ra pondered this. And then she smiled.

"Uh-oh," said Han.

At Jenra's questioning look, Han explained, "That's Qi'ra's 'I'm coming up with a plan' face."

"Oh?" She turned to Qi'ra. "Are you? Coming up with a plan?"

Qi'ra couldn't stop smiling.

CHAPTER 18

Han had to shake himself loose from the snare of Qi'ra's smile. That smile did funny things to his head. For instance, earlier it had actually made him believe for a moment that he could pilot a starship someday.

Good thing he'd come to his senses fast.

"I know you're having trouble finding buyers who will risk the Empire's wrath without betraying you," Qi'ra was saying to the Engineer. "But I know someone who can find them for you."

"Who?" Han prompted.

Tsuulo let his head fall into his hands. He'd obviously figured it out already.

"Lady Proxima."

Han frowned. "Not this again. Qi'ra, I've already told you, she doesn't care about us. She just—"

Qi'ra put up a hand to forestall his protests. "Hear me out. If we—"

But Jenra said, "Wait. Last time, Proxima's bid was the lowest. Insultingly low. Does she have any idea what she's doing?"

"She had no idea what your shield tech was worth," Qi'ra said. "But she knows everyone on Corellia."

Han was warming to the idea. "As gangs go, the White Worms are nothing compared to one of the big syndicates," he said. "But Qi'ra's right. Lady Proxima knows everyone. The White Worms have deep roots on Corellia. Old roots. Proxima has more influence than money. She has connections."

Tsuulo said, "And guards."

"And guards," Han added. "She has a whole army of White Worms, so she can make any meeting location secure. There's no chance of the Kaldana Syndicate showing up and trying to blast their way to a winning bid again."

"She can broker the deal for you," Qi'ra said. "She can rally buyers, arrange payment and delivery, and keep everything secure. All under the Empire's nose. For a small commission, of course."

Jenra's eyes narrowed. "How much of a commission?"

Qi'ra hesitated.

Han knew that if she picked a number that was too low, she risked being insulting again. But if she picked a number that was too high, Jenra would never take the deal seriously.

"One half of one percent of the gross sale price."

Jenra raised a single eyebrow. "Hmmm."

Han did the math in his head. If the Engineer received another bid as high as the last one—a billion credits—then Lady Proxima and the White Worms would come away from the deal with a cool five million. That was more money than Han had ever seen in his life.

"You know exactly what Proxima bid the last time," Qi'ra said. "So you know that's a lot of money for her. But it's nothing for you. Both of you win."

"What's in it for you three?" Jenra asked. "What do you win?"

Han and Qi'ra looked at each other, and understanding passed between them. Tsuulo's face was still in his hands.

"We get to go home," Qi'ra said softly. "Such as it is."

"It's not like we have anywhere else to go," Han said.

"People like us don't survive down there without joining a gang or a syndicate," Qi'ra said.

Han knew exactly what Qi'ra meant by "people like us." People with no family, no friends, no resources.

"Proxima saves face," Han added. "And she lets us back into the White Worms as heroes who saved the day and made her rich."

Han could tell he sounded as glum as he felt. Two days before, he would have done anything to go back to the White Worms safely, resume his hardscrabble life of running errands for Lady Proxima while secretly working on his junker speeder. But now . . .

He stared out the window. The stars looked so different from up here than planetside, where clouds and smog and light pollution made a starry night as rare as a beautiful day. He'd always known in his head that the galaxy was a big place. But now he knew it in his gut, in his very being. There were billions of stars out there, maybe more, and he wanted to see them all.

"I suppose it's worth a try," the Engineer said at last, and her face was smug. Han had a feeling she'd gotten exactly what she wanted. Maybe that was why she was being so nice; she needed someone from Corellia to broker the deal. Naturally, Qi'ra had figured it out and taken advantage.

"Now we contact Proxima?" Han asked.

Jenra stood. "Come with me. My comm room on level three is equipped with a holotransceiver."

Tsuulo finally looked up, eyes bright. He didn't want to miss the opportunity to see a new gadget at work.

They followed Jenra out of the viewing lounge, down a short corridor to a lift. As they walked, he couldn't help noticing the way Qi'ra was staring straight ahead, her face a mask of frozen perfection. That meant something was bothering her, but no way was she going to let on.

He leaned over and whispered, "This was a good idea."

"I guess." She frowned thoughtfully. "I mean, thanks."

It took a while to coordinate with Lady Proxima. Jenra didn't trust any of the standard Corellian transmission frequencies, so she had to contact the White Worm leader using assets on the ground, then arrange a secure line of communication. All that logistical stuff seemed boring to Han, but Qi'ra and Tsuulo drank it in—Qi'ra for the strategizing, Tsuulo for the tech.

Eventually, they worked it out, and Han found himself in the comm room with Jenra and his friends, staring at a pedestal. Atop the pedestal was a flat metal circle, studded with what looked like glass coins.

"Projectors," Tsuulo whispered to him.

Jenra operated the console, firing it up. A form buzzed to life on the pedestal before them, glowing blue, hunchbacked with a beakish face and cloudy, wide-spaced eyes.

Lady Proxima.

"Han. Qi'ra. Tsuulo. My darling children," she crooned. "It's such a relief to see you all safe and hale." The holotransceiver displayed the White Worm leader at only three-quarter size, but Han still fought the urge to recoil. "And you must be the Engineer I've heard so much about."

Jenra inclined her head in acknowledgment but said nothing.

"It's lovely to see you, my lady," Qi'ra answered smoothly, but her hands were clutched tightly before her.

"Moloch and his scrumrats, Rebolt and his hounds, they've been all over Coronet City, looking for you, hoping to bring you home safely," Proxima said. "Everyone is just so worried."

"Yeah, we've been worried too," said Han wryly. "Worried we were going to die."

Qi'ra shot him a warning glance.

"Well, I don't deny that there is much I wished to discuss with you," Proxima said. "Regarding that absolute debacle of an assignment. Perhaps our eagerness to retrieve you was misinterpreted."

Fat chance of that, but this time Han kept his mouth shut and let Qi'ra take the lead.

"Speaking of our assignment," she said, "we asked the Engineer to contact you for us so that we could complete it."

Lady Proxima blinked, and the fingers of her left hand twitched. "You wish to complete your assignment," she said flatly.

"Yes, my lady." Quickly, Qi'ra sketched out the plan.

Han admired the way she did it, adding lots of flattery about Proxima's connections and influence, setting up the next idea and then dragging her heels just long enough that Proxima would suggest it herself—and think of it as her own. His own style was more direct and on the nose, the way a punch was on the nose. He could never do things the way Qi'ra did them.

"If you bring serious buyers to the deal and guarantee their discretion, the Engineer will award you a broker's fee," Qi'ra finished.

Lady Proxima's eyes widened. Her fingers were twitching in earnest now. "And how big is the broker's fee?"

"Based on the largest offer last time, it would be ten times the amount proffered by the White Worms," Qi'ra said.

Proxima's eyes narrowed and she leaned forward. The faint sound of her clicking came across the holoprojection like a burst of static. "What percent is that?"

"One half of one percent of the sale price."

Lady Proxima recoiled as if she'd been physically struck by the size of the other bids.

Tsuulo tugged on Qi'ra's sleeve and whispered something in her ear, and Han only caught the words for "home" and "White Worms" and "kill." Han prepared to translate, but Qi'ra must have understood fine because she said, "Tsuulo reminds me: your commission is contingent upon you welcoming us back into the White Worms. You must agree that there will be no repercussions for . . . er, how long it took to complete our assignment."

Lady Proxima pretended to consider, but Han could tell she was sold.

"So that's all? I arrange buyers and let you back into the White Worms?"

"And you have to double our food rations!" Han blurted. "Not just us. For all the scrumrats. With the money you're about to make, you can afford it, easy."

"Yes, what Han said," Qi'ra affirmed calmly, although she sent a quick glance and the flicker of a smile his way.

"And you, Madame Engineer," Proxima said. "You've negotiated with my children and agreed to these terms?"

"I have," Jenra said. "They are exceptional children. You should be proud."

"Let's make it six-tenths of a percent."

"Five-and-a-half-tenths."

"Deal."

Lady Proxima opened her wide beak mouth in what passed for a grin. "I'll get to work right away. Expect me to contact you on this frequency in exactly one Corellian day. And, Qi'ra, my darling . . . this had better work. If not, I'll—"

"We look forward to hearing from you," Jenra said.

She hit a switch, and the projection of Lady Proxima flickered out. "Is she always so horrible?"

"Horribler," Qi'ra said.

"She's the horriblest," Han said.

"All in all, I think that went well," the Engineer said. "Let's hope she comes through."

"She will," Han assured her. "There's no way she's letting all that money slip her grasp."

Qi'ra wiped her hands on her skirt and took a deep breath.

"Were you nervous?" Han said.

"Maybe a little."

"Well, you did great."

"Thanks, you too. And thanks, Tsuulo, for suggesting we make our return an official part of the deal."

Tsuulo bleeped happily about the Force being with them.

"I guess we have a day to kill," Han said. "Can I maybe have that tour of the ship now?"

Jenra smiled indulgently. "I'll have my assistant show you around."

Han turned for the door. If this was his last day on an actual starship, he was going to make the most of it.

"Wait, Qi'ra," the Engineer said. "I'd like a word with you."

They all stopped.

"Just Qi'ra," Jenra clarified.

Han had a bad feeling. And Qi'ra did too, judging by her narrow-eyed, cornered-rat demeanor.

"Whatever you say to me, you can say in front of my . . . friends," Qi'ra said.

Jenra shrugged. "Very well. I could use another assistant. Someone qualified to be my spokesperson, who will negotiate and entertain on my behalf on those occasions when it would be best not to show my face. I'm on the run from the Empire, after all."

Qi'ra's lips parted in surprise. Han felt the walls of the comm room closing in around him.

"You'll need training," Jenra continued blithely. "Definitely some grooming. But I believe you have tremendous potential."

Qi'ra just stared. Tsuulo started jabbering about what a good spokesperson Qi'ra would be.

"What's he saying?" Jenra asked.

"He says Qi'ra would be perfect for the job," Han translated, and his words sounded far away, as if they were coming from someone else. Why was it suddenly so hot in here? He tugged on his vest, trying to loosen it.

"And what do *you* think, young Han?" Jenra asked.

"I think . . ." He could hardly get enough air. "I think Tsuulo's right. Qi'ra can do anything, become anyone. That's just who she is."

"High praise indeed," Jenra said. She turned back to Qi'ra, who hadn't moved, much less said a word. She was like a frozen statue, or maybe a bird poised to take flight. "You remind me of myself, Qi'ra. When I was younger. Full of ideas and ambition, but short on opportunity. In another life, on another world, you might have been an engineer like me."

Still, Qi'ra said nothing.

Tsuulo's sturdier antenna drooped. Han remembered that he'd hoped to be an engineer himself someday.

Jenra pressed on. "You'd never lack for food. Or nice clothes. You'd see the galaxy. Surely life aboard the *Red Nimbus* is better than the one waiting for you back in the sewers."

Qi'ra should accept. She'd be stupid not to. Right?

Finally, she spoke. "What about my friends?"

Jenra smiled coldly, in a way that Han thought was really no smile at all. "I don't need three more assistants. Just one."

"But what . . . what about . . ."

"Oh, my sweet, young girl, if you want better things—and I've been watching you; I know you do—you have to make sacrifices. That means leaving friends behind. They have their own futures. No doubt to rise high in the hierarchy of Lady Proxima's little gang. We all take different paths. This is the one laid out before you."

Qi'ra opened her mouth. Closed it.

"I would have offered it to you privately," Jenra said. "But you insisted that I do it in front of your . . . friends."

Qi'ra looked to Tsuulo, and then Han, as if seeking answers. Or maybe permission.

Han pictured it in his mind: Going back to the White Worms. Descending into the sewers. Faithfully tinkering on his speeder that didn't even have an engine yet. Running errands for Proxima day in and day out. Eating rat sludge.

All without Qi'ra. After today, he might never see her again.

He whirled angrily and headed out the door. He threw the words over his shoulder like weapons: "I'll give you your privacy. I'm sure you have lots to discuss without me. I'll find your assistant myself. Finally take that tour."

CHAPTER 19

Qi'ra watched Han leave the viewing lounge, feeling a sickness that had nothing to do with eating too much rich food. Tsuulo twittered something and left a moment later.

"That boy really likes you," the Engineer said.

Qi'ra shrugged, trying to appear nonchalant. "We've been through a lot together the past few days."

"Is that why you're hesitant to accept my offer? Don't let a boy hold you back, Qi'ra. The galaxy is full of boys, even attractive ones like Han."

"I'll keep that in mind."

"Are you saying you need time?"

"Yes, that's exactly what I'm saying." Qi'ra wanted to be alone more than anything in the galaxy. She needed to think. The Engineer's offer of employment was the most incredible thing that had ever happened to her. But something about it wasn't right. And she couldn't say what.

"Well, you only have a day. Then I'm gone."

Qi'ra's shock was wearing off, her survival instinct

kicking back in. She realized she needed to say something placating. "I understand. And . . . thank you. It's a
very generous offer."

She fled—walked purposefully—out of the viewing
lounge and didn't take a breath until the doors slid shut
behind her and she was standing in the corridor.

Everything she had ever wanted, and more, offered
to her on a silver platter.

And she had *earned* it.

She had earned this opportunity, not once, but over
and over again.

So why was she hesitating?

The Engineer was wrong about one thing—it wasn't
because she was interested in a boy. Not that way.

But there was something about Han, something that
she had learned by watching him these past few days, and
she was still trying to figure it out.

Is this a gut instinct? she wondered.

No, she was pretty sure that the only thing her gut
was telling her was that she'd eaten too many buttered
biscuits. This was her head trying to tell her something,
but it was like listening to Tsuulo talk: when the words
and ideas came too fast, she couldn't keep up.

A protocol droid came down the corridor and
paused beside her. "Mistress Qi'ra? May I help you find
something?"

"My friends were taking a tour," she said. "I would like to join them."

"Of course. This way please."

She found Tsuulo right where she expected him—hunkered down with the ship's engineers, asking questions at approximately the speed of light. One of the other engineers was a turquoise-colored Rodian, a woman with a broom of emerald-green hair. Tsuulo looked genuinely happy, maybe for the first time since she'd met him.

Qi'ra didn't want to disturb him, so she kept on walking.

Han was in the cockpit of the ship, sitting in the copilot's chair beside the Wookiee, Roo. She could only see the back of Han's head because he was staring out into space like a man ready to go places. He was probably as happy as Tsuulo.

Then Roo said something, and Han turned his head.

There was a deep sadness written on his profile. A few days before, she might not have noticed, because it was subtle: a brightness missing from his eyes, shoulders that lacked their usual jauntiness.

Like Tsuulo, he was engaged in an animated discussion. She might understand a little Huttese, but she couldn't pick up a single word of Shyriiwook. From the amount of Han's gesturing, and Roo's head shaking and nodding, it seemed Han didn't know many words either but was quickly picking them up. He said something, and Roo tilted his head back, giving a great barking laugh.

That was it. . . .

That was why she was thinking about Han. Over the past few days, Han had treated everyone they encountered like a person. Powlo. Tsuulo. Tool. Roo. Even her. Especially her. She felt like Han looked past the surface things that everyone saw and recognized her as worthy of respect.

How did the Engineer describe Roo? *My most valuable asset.*

That was the problem.

If Qi'ra decided to accept the Engineer's offer, she would stop being a person. She would become another asset, of greater or lesser value. She fully expected it to be of greater value, but how much value could one assistant have when Jenra was getting ready to close a deal for a billion credits? None. She would be as replaceable as a duct rat working in the Foundry.

On the other hand, if she accepted, she would be so much better off than she was now. She could save some money. Even invest. She would have opportunities that she would never have as Head for Lady Proxima, or even running her own gang on Corellia. She wouldn't have to stay Jenra's assistant forever. She could do it for a while, learn, then go her own way.

Her choice was suddenly much clearer.

If only her answer were too.

Maybe she should ask Han to help her figure things out. But no, he'd been angry and brusque, and anyway she didn't want to interrupt his conversation.

Roo was pointing out controls and showing Han how to use them. She'd seen Han pilot a speeder, and she knew he belonged on a ship like this one. There was no way she would steal this moment from him.

Silently, she turned away and went back to their bunk room. When the two boys returned many hours later, she pretended to be asleep. Even after Tsuulo started snoring, she lay awake in the darkness, making plans.

No matter what choice she made, it created different options and opportunities. The possibilities spun out in her head, becoming the glowing blue lines of those plans, heading in endless directions—stunningly beautiful to contemplate, but no matter how hard she tried, she couldn't read them at all.

Han was gently shaking her awake. "Come on," he said. "The Engineer has summoned us back to the viewing lounge."

Qi'ra jumped out of bed. They proceeded to the lounge in unusual silence, lost in their own thoughts.

When they entered the lounge, a buffet was spread out just like the previous day, with just as many choices, if not quite as many servings. She didn't have an appetite and neither did Tsuulo. Han grabbed a pastry as he passed the bar, but didn't seem to have a lot of enthusiasm for eating it.

Jenra awaited them. She wore a gown of sapphire blue this time, and her hair was unbound, framing her face like a huge dark halo. "I've spoken with Lady Proxima," she said as they entered.

"Is the auction going forward?" Qi'ra asked.

"It already has. You were right about her contacts and her ability to move swiftly. Proxima was true to her word. There were four buyers this time, two of whom you are already familiar with."

"The Droid Gotra and the Kaldana Syndicate," Han said.

"Indeed. The Gotra stuck with their original bid. One billion credits. But this time the Kaldana offered one point one billion."

Han whistled.

Qi'ra quickly calculated Lady Proxima's percentage. Six million, fifty thousand credits. The old woman was rich beyond her greediest dreams, thanks to Qi'ra, Han, and Tsuulo.

"So the Kaldana Syndicate wins," Qi'ra said. Han

was probably unhappy about that. He had a soft spot for that droid friend of his.

Sure enough, Han said, "You could give the cube to the Droid Gotra anyway."

Jenra blinked. "Why would I do that?"

"For a good cause. The Kaldana will use your technology to terrorize neighboring systems. No one will be safe."

"I care nothing for causes. That extra hundred million credits will go a long way."

"Surely there's more to it than just money?" Qi'ra asked.

"Of course," Jenra said. "What I really want is freedom. To explore the galaxy. Or to settle down somewhere on the Outer Rim. I want to create my designs in peace and sell them to whomever I choose. But here's the thing, sweet girl: money *is* freedom."

Tsuulo chattered at them, and Han translated: "He says giving it to the droids is the right thing to do. It's what the Force would want."

That made no sense to Qi'ra. "Are you saying the Force is some kind of god?"

Tsuulo shook his head, muttering in frustration.

"Not exactly," Han said. "And actually, he's changing his mind. He read that the Force moves through living creatures, so he doesn't know if it has anything to do with droids or not. He just knows that giving the shield tech to the Gotra feels like the right thing."

Jenra turned her back to them and gazed out at the stars. The edges of one of the asteroids had rotated into view. It was just one asteroid, a speck of dust on the galaxy-wide scale, yet it dwarfed the *Red Nimbus*. "And what do you think, Qi'ra?" she asked.

"I think it's impractical to make a big decision based on a feeling."

"I agree," the Engineer said.

"But there are some practical reasons to keep that tech out of Kaldana hands."

"Oh?"

"Like Han said, if the Kaldana get it, the Corellia system becomes almost un-flyable. They're already a major player here. With this technology, they will crush their competition and start spreading to other systems." Qi'ra felt herself warming to the topic. The stakes were huge. So much bigger than anything she'd dealt with before. The consequences of this deal had the potential to reach galaxy-wide. And she was right in the middle of it. For better or worse, she had helped make this happen. For today at least, she was a major player.

"Why give them the resources to take their operations galaxy-wide?" Qi'ra continued. "Do you really want to upset the balance of power like that?"

"Maybe I do," Jenra said. "It might keep the Empire busy for a while. Off my back."

"I can't blame you for that," Qi'ra said. "I mean, if I were you, I'd just want to survive."

Han said, "I really think you should give it to the droids."

"Me too," Tsuulo said, and Qi'ra understood his words clear as day.

Jenra turned to face them, her sapphire gown swishing at her heels. How many incredible gowns did she own? "I made my decision hours ago. The Kaldana ship will be here any moment. Lady Proxima assured me that the three of you would complete the exchange in person. After that, the Kaldana will escort you safely back to Coronet City."

"Whoa," said Han. "The Kaldana are coming here?"

"We're doing the exchange?" Qi'ra said.

Tsuulo protested too, but all Qi'ra caught was the world for "kill."

He was a handy fellow to have around, because in spite of their broken communication, Tsuulo always managed to get her thinking. And right now, she was thinking that the Engineer wanted to be rid of them after all. Her hospitality and kindness had been a ruse. Maybe even her job offer. Jenra was not going to let them go, not really. She was washing her hands of them and sending them to the Kaldana.

Maybe the Kaldana would let them live. But if they didn't, Jenra wasn't going to lose any sleep. Because she was at heart a betrayer. In the end, no one mattered to Jenra except Jenra.

And people like Qi'ra and Han and Tsuulo? They were assets, and of limited value.

It was as though the Engineer had read her mind, because she said, "Qi'ra, my offer is still on the table. You have a place here on the *Red Nimbus* if you want it. The boys can handle the exchange."

So maybe the job offer wasn't a ruse. Everything in Qi'ra screamed to accept. Avoid going to the Kaldana ship. She'd have food, beautiful clothes, something important to do. She'd *live*.

Qi'ra opened her mouth to say yes, but the word lodged in her throat. Finally, she managed, "I guess I'm still thinking about it."

Jenra was about to say something else, but Han pointed toward the window. "I think the Kaldana ship is here," he said.

The ugliest starship Qi'ra had ever seen glided into view. It was huge, easily three times the size of the *Red Nimbus*, with jagged protrusions and pointed attachments.

Blaster burns scorched its side, and the pulse engine belched a plume of dirty gray exhaust.

"That thing is a beast," Han said, eyes wide. "It looks like they slapped the power converter on with just a few screws and some adhesive. And their pulse engine is burning hard fuel. A ship that size should have been retrofitted a long time ago."

Tsuulo barked something, gesturing angrily.

"Yeah, an abomination. I've never seen an ion flux stabilizer that looks like that before. How did they put together such a huge bid if they can't even afford proper ship maintenance and upgrades?"

"They sold their flagship," Jenra said, looking amused. "To help cover the cost of their bid. This is the junker they bought to replace it."

"Oh," Han breathed. "They *really* want that shield tech."

"In any case, grab all your belongings and prepare to board," Jenra ordered. "We'll be docking together via airlock in a moment."

They all looked at each other and shrugged. They'd come with nothing more than the clothes on their backs and Tsuulo's datapad, and that was what they'd leave with. Qi'ra eyed the bar, and all the platters of food laid wastefully across it. Too bad they couldn't take bucket-loads of food with them.

Han and Tsuulo were staring at her, and it took a moment for her to realize why: she still hadn't given Jenra an answer.

"Let's go," Qi'ra said gruffly. "To the airlock."

CHAPTER 20

So Qi'ra was coming with them instead of staying behind? Why would she give up all this to go back to the sewers with Lady Proxima?

Han didn't understand it. But as they walked from the viewing lounge to the passenger dock, he was afraid to mention it, or even speak to her, in case she came to her senses and changed her mind.

A hollow clang sounded as the extending airlock tunnel hit the hull of the *Red Nimbus*. Magnets sealed it in place, then air hissed while the pressure and atmosphere stabilized inside. The hatch opened before them.

Jenra produced the datacube and handed it to Qi'ra. "I'll leave this in your care."

"Tsuulo?" He stepped forward, and Qi'ra handed him the cube. "You've carried it this far. Might as well go all the way."

"Thank you," he said solemnly.

She replied, "You're welcome," before Han had a chance to translate.

This was it. The sign he'd been waiting for. Qi'ra was

staying. She'd handed the cube to Tsuulo because she wouldn't be joining them on the Kaldana ship.

He should be happy for her. She'd get off of Corellia, see the far reaches of the galaxy, and have a chance to use and develop her talents in ways he suspected he couldn't fully grasp. But he didn't like it. He couldn't say why, exactly, just that he had a very bad feeling about Qi'ra taking that job.

"You're to hand it over, then wait for them to confirm the contents," Jenra explained, primarily to Qi'ra, but with one eye on Tsuulo. "After that, they'll transfer money—to both me and Lady Proxima. Once I've received the money, I'll transmit the encryption key. Then they'll escort you to a shuttle and fly you back down to Corellia. I don't know if the shuttle is equipped with a hyperdrive, so it might be a long journey, but you'll get home eventually."

"That doesn't sound too complicated," Han said.

Tsuulo held the cube between his thumb and forefinger, staring at it. He was holding more than a billion credits' worth of merchandise in his hand. Han wanted to remember this moment.

The far end of the airlock hissed open, revealing a young woman in Kaldana black. Han was glad to note that her blaster remained holstered. If he made it back to Corellia alive, he was going to acquire a blaster somehow.

It wasn't fair that he kept showing up to blaster fights armed with luck and charm.

"Last chance, Qi'ra," Jenra said.

They all looked at her. Han's heart was in his throat.

"I . . ." Qi'ra couldn't keep the emotion from her face. Her brow was knit, her lips parted.

Han tried to find a little sympathy but couldn't. He wanted to scream at her not to stay on the *Red Nimbus*. He wanted to hit something.

Finally, Tsuulo said in the softest voice Han had ever heard from him, "I will miss you, Qi'ra, my friend."

Han didn't know if Qi'ra understood, but she looked at Tsuulo, then at Han, and back to Tsuulo, who suddenly reached his arms out, drew her close, and embraced her soundly. Qi'ra remained stiff in Tsuulo's arms for the space of a breath. Then, to Han's very great surprise, Qi'ra hugged the little Rodian right back.

Then Qi'ra extricated herself, turned to the Engineer. Did Han imagine that her eyes were moist with tears? "I'm sorry," she said. "I won't leave my friends."

Han felt all the air return to his lungs. But Jenra shrugged like it was no big deal. "In that case, I wish you all the very best." She turned to go, leaving them in the entrance to the airlock.

Qi'ra stepped forward, ready to be the first one through.

Suddenly, Jenra whirled back around, gripped Qi'ra by the shoulders, and pulled her close to whisper something in her ear.

Qi'ra's eyes narrowed thoughtfully.

The Engineer stepped away, but their gazes remained locked. Qi'ra nodded some kind of understanding.

Then Jenra disappeared into the bowels of her yacht, and a voice behind them said, "Come on, we haven't got all day."

The three of them stepped through the airlock.

"This way," the Kaldana woman said. "Everyone's waiting for you in the conference room."

The insides of the Kaldana ship were as ugly as the outsides. The corridors were small and crowded with cargo boxes, tools, gear, even a few sleeping pallets. The lights flickered on and off, indicative of an engine problem.

Qi'ra's eyes took in everything, as though memorizing it all. She was concentrating so hard she almost tripped over a sleeping pallet. Or maybe she had just pretended to trip, because it brought the two of them head-to-head.

Han grabbed the sleeve of her jacket. He whispered, "What did Jenra say to you back there?"

Qi'ra yanked Tsuulo close. Talking fast and low, she said, "We need to escape from this ship as soon as possible. Once the exchange is made, Jenra thinks we should run for it."

Tsuulo swore.

"She thinks the Kaldana will kill us," Han whispered back.

"Probably," Qi'ra said. "She gave me one of those gas bomb thingies. It's in my pocket."

"But we have no breather masks this time," Han pointed out.

"Nope."

"We need an escape route."

"Hey, enough with the committee," the Kaldana woman barked. "Are we doing this exchange or not?"

Qi'ra moved to follow her, saying under her breath, "Help me memorize the layout. Keep an eye out for decent cover. And escape pods."

"I remember seeing a jettison hatch from the viewing window," Han said. "It was aft, near the pulse engine."

"That's a terrible place for an escape pod," Tsuulo said.

"The worst."

"Oh! I know exactly where it is!" Qi'ra blurted, a little too loud.

"Are you sure?"

"Have I ever let you down?"

As they hurried down the cluttered corridor, Han considered that finding an escape pod might be the easy part. Their bigger problem was that, given the way this ship was maintained, there was a chance the pod hadn't been serviced in years. It might not work at all.

The Kaldana woman led them through a branching corridor, up in a lift, and to a doorway. The door no longer functioned; it was covered with a thick red velvet curtain that was blotchy and stained with something Han preferred not to know about.

She swept up the curtain and ushered them inside.

The "conference room" was actually a small hold with a high ceiling, a freight lift, and a grease-stained floor studded with bolts for lashing down cargo. But instead of cargo, the hold was filled with cheap furniture—a few ratty couches, two armchairs, some scattered tables, all secured to the floor with cargo straps. Kaldana Syndicate thugs were everywhere, lounging with their boots up, sipping Corellian ale. One group off to the side was playing a version of sabacc that used a couple of dice.

Han almost liked this room. A fellow could relax in a place like this, put his feet up. But if he ever got a ship of his own, he'd keep it clean. In tip-top shape. No ale spills, no gear scattered in the corridors, and definitely no bulkheads replaced by curtains. Han would take care of his ship. Treat it with the respect it deserved.

A man rose from the couch. Like the rest, he wore all

black except for the Kaldana triangle on his upper arm. His long black hair was pulled back into a ponytail, and gold studs shone from piercings in his ears and nostrils.

"Why'd you bring *that* on board my ship?" he said, glaring at Tsuulo. Everyone else in the hold was staring at them. A few hands twitched toward their holstered blasters.

Han instinctively shifted a little closer to his friend, noting that Qi'ra did the same.

"There's a problem?" Qi'ra said.

"Aliens are always a problem," the captain said. "Especially Rodians. Those little slimeballs are the scourge of the galaxy. Can't do honest business anymore without ending up with a Rodian bounty hunter on your tail."

Tsuulo muttered darkly, something about wishing poisoned bowels upon the Kaldana and all their spawn for a hundred generations.

"What?" the captain demanded. "What did it say?"

"*He* said we should get on with our business," Qi'ra said.

Come to think of it, Han had yet to see a Kaldana thug who wasn't human. That explained a lot. No wonder the Kaldana were going to such lengths to keep Jenra's shield tech out of the hands of the Droid Gotra. They hated anything and anyone who wasn't human.

"You have the cube?" the captain asked.

"You have the credit transfer ready?" Qi'ra asked.

"I do."

"Then we do too." She turned. "Tsuulo?"

He pulled the datacube from his pocket but had barely begun to offer it before the captain dashed forward and snatched it from his fingers.

The captain handed it off to one of his thugs, who plugged it into a datapad. Holographic lines and flowing text filled the air of the cargo hold, lighting faces and furniture. Even the sabacc players paused their game to look up.

"Seems legitimate," said the thug. The captain nodded at him, and the thug pulled the cube from the datapad and stashed it, returning the hold to its previous gloom.

"Now the transfer," Han prompted. He looked down at Qi'ra, who mouthed, *Be ready.*

The thug tapped out a code. He offered the datapad to the captain, who reviewed the screen and then pressed his thumbprint to the reader. Something flashed.

"There," said the thug. "Six million and fifty thousand credits to Proxima, the rest to the Engineer."

"Now we wait," said the captain. He crossed his arms over his chest and stared at them. Especially Tsuulo.

Han hated waiting, and he hated awkward silences. "Nice ship you got here," he said.

"Shut up, kid," the captain snapped.

Okay, screw it. "Actually, this ship is a piece of junk," Han said. "Maybe the ugliest I've seen. I can't believe she actually flies."

Qi'ra elbowed him. "Han, what are you doing?" she whispered.

"At least I have a ship," the captain said. "What's a scrumrat like you know about flying?"

"Enough to know that putting your power converter outside your hull means you have environmental problems. Does your crew realize they could die any day?"

The captain grinned. The thug grinned. A woman rose from the sofa, hand on her blaster, and Han nearly stepped back, startled. It was the woman from the Foundry, the one who'd betrayed them all and attacked Tool. She was grinning too.

The captain yelled, "What kind of day is it, Kaldana?"

They slammed their heels together and lifted their right forefingers in salute. "A good day to die!" they yelled back in chorus, their voices thundering.

It was some kind of rallying cry, and Han had walked right into it. The sentiment proved one thing: once this transfer went through, the Kaldana were going to start shooting. He was sure of it.

"So," the captain said. He put a foot up on one of the tables and rested his forearm on his knee. "Have you three had a chance to study the plans?"

Han hooked his thumbs at himself and opened his eyes wide. "Us? No, of course not."

"Those are plans?" Qi'ra asked. "I thought they were pretty lines."

"You mean the cube doesn't store celestial music?" Tsuulo asked, and Han was glad no one but him could understand.

"It came through," the thug said. "We have the encryption key."

Han started to back toward the curtain that covered their exit, hoping his friends would follow.

"You're not going anywhere," the captain said, and Han froze. "Not until we're sure this works."

"Wow," said Qi'ra. "I'm literally *holding my breath* in suspense."

The captain gave her a strange look.

"She takes her deal exchanges very seriously," Han said, preparing to hold his breath. He hoped Tsuulo had understood Qi'ra's message too.

The thug threw up his hands in triumph. "It worked! We got it!"

A cheer rose from everyone gathered. Backs were slapped, bottles of ale were clinked, and one man collapsed against the sofa like the weight of the galaxy had just lifted from his shoulders.

Qi'ra cleared her throat. When all eyes were on her,

she said, "We'd like an escort to our shuttle now."

Her right hand was inside her jacket pocket.

Han began to breathe deeply through his nose, preparing his lungs for the torture to come.

"You seem like good kids," the captain said. "I'm sorry we have to do this. But we can't leave any loose ends. I'm sure you understand. You've seen our faces, our ship, those plans."

Han's hands went up in what he hoped was a gesture of surrender. "We saw nothing. We were never here."

The captain shook his head. He seemed truly regretful. "Sewer rats like you sell information cheap. We can't take the chance."

He pulled his blaster from his holster and flicked a release, changing the setting from "stun" to "kill."

Qi'ra yanked the gas bomb from her pocket.

Han held his breath.

The captain aimed for his head.

Qi'ra engaged the switch and tossed the metal sphere into the air.

"What the . . ."

A split-second distraction was all they needed. They turned and sprinted for the curtained doorway.

Blaster fire erupted around them, but it was messy and unfocused.

"Watch the gas!" someone yelled.

"Take cover!" yelled another.

Han reached the curtain first. He yanked it aside and ushered Tsuulo and Qi'ra through. A blaster bolt singed his hair as he ducked through after them.

Fleeing while holding one's breath was even more torturous than he'd anticipated. His lungs burned. Spots danced in his vision. His heart pumped so hard and fast he thought it might tumble from his chest.

Qi'ra turned a corner and bent over gasping. Tsuulo and Han nearly collided with her back. They spent a precious moment sucking in air.

"You think that worked?" Qi'ra asked.

"I don't hear blaster fire anymore," Han said.

"That cargo hold was a lot bigger than the room we were in the last time we set off one of those," Tsuulo said. "The gas won't be as concentrated, and it might not have affected everyone."

Han translated for Qi'ra, who said, "And you can bet one or two of them were quick-thinking enough to hold their breath and get out of its range. Plus we don't know how many of them are on the rest of this ship."

"Let's find an escape pod," Han said.

"That's the plan." Qi'ra turned and sprinted down the corridor. "Follow me!"

"You know where we're going?" Han said, still breathless.

"Yes!" she called over her shoulder. "A schematic of the ship was posted on the wall. Saw it earlier."

That meant this ship had once been a fully compliant, regulation freighter, before someone had desecrated it. Well, that was lucky. But there was more to it than just luck—Qi'ra had known to look for the schematics and had the presence of mind to memorize what she saw.

A spark of hope blossomed inside him. They could do this.

Then a ship-wide alarm began wailing, and the corridor they traveled pulsed with red light.

Tsuulo swore.

"You were right, Qi'ra," Han yelled. "Someone escaped that gas."

"There's the lift," Qi'ra hollered. "Get in, quick."

They tumbled inside. Footsteps pounded nearby. A half dozen Kaldana pirates turned a corner and bore down on them.

They raised their blasters.

The lift closed, and blaster fire dented the door.

Qi'ra punched deck three, and they lurched upward.

"Too close," Tsuulo said.

"Deck three is mostly maintenance access," Qi'ra said. "I'm hoping it won't be fully occupied."

"People could still be waiting for us, so be ready," said Han.

The lift door slid open, revealing a dark corridor lit only by the red alarm light. Junk was piled everywhere— spare parts, old furniture, bits of armor, a tool cart. But no people.

They stepped outside. "Hold the door," Qi'ra ordered Tsuulo. Then to Han: "Help me shove all this stuff inside the lift. Everything that can fit. Hurry!"

They complied. Han worked as fast as he could, lifting and heaving junk into the lift. When it could hold no more, they pushed the tool cart partway inside so it blocked the door.

"There," Qi'ra said, looking smug. "Even if they get that lift working, there won't be room for anyone to ride it."

"Smart," Han said. "Now let's go! Quietly now."

Her eyes brightened with the compliment, but she hurried down the corridor on light feet, the boys following after. They paused at every junction to peek around the corner, making sure no one was in sight before continuing on.

"There has to be another lift," Tsuulo whispered.

"Yeah, this ship is too big for just one turbolift," Han said.

"It's on the port side," Qi'ra whispered. "The Kaldana will get up here eventually, so stay alert."

Qi'ra led them around a corner, and smack-dab into a sealed bulkhead.

"Blast," she said.

Han tried the access panel, but nothing happened. "Now what?"

"Move over," ordered Tsuulo. He whipped a cable from his pack and attached one end to his datapad, the other to the terminal beside the access panel. "You know what would be great right now?" Tsuulo said, even has he keyed into his datapad. "A scomp link. Or better yet, an astromech droid."

"Hurry," said Qi'ra. "I think someone's coming."

The access panel whirred with activity.

Running footsteps approached. From somewhere close by came the sound of clutter being kicked aside. "This way!" someone said.

"Tsuulo . . ." Han whispered.

"I just have to believe I can do it," Tsuulo was muttering. "Almost got it. C'mon, Force, help me out. . . . There!"

The bulkhead slid open.

Blaster fire erupted all around them. The air smelled of ozone and burned fabric.

Qi'ra raced through, and Tsuulo tried to follow but stumbled.

"On your feet!" Han yelled, yanking him up by his

shirt and shoving him through the doorway. Together they tumbled to the floor. Qi'ra smashed her palm against the access panel, and the bulkhead slammed down behind them.

"There's no lock," she said. "We have to run for it."

"Something's wrong with Tsuulo," Han said.

The Rodian wasn't getting up. His legs were splayed across the floor, his head lolling. But his hand still gripped that datapad as if it were life itself.

"C'mon, pal, on your feet," Han said, tugging at Tsuulo's arm, but he wouldn't budge.

"Tsuulo, we have to go!" Qi'ra said.

The Rodian reached slowly with his free hand, pulled back his jacket, and revealed a gaping, steaming wound in his side. A blaster had caught him from behind, taking a chunk of his back and stomach. Blood dripped on the floor around him.

"Oh," said Qi'ra. "Oh, no."

Han's stomach clenched. The sight . . . the smell . . . He closed his mind to it and reached for his friend. "Fine, I'll carry you. We'll get you out of—"

"Stop," Tsuulo whispered. He lifted his datapad toward Han. "Take it. You'll need it. Access escape pod."

"What? No! We need *you* to do that. If you let me carry—"

"Just believe you can do it," Tsuulo said. His voice

was growing weaker. He waved the datapad, the cable still dangling. "Take it!"

Han took it. "Tsuulo . . ."

"I was wrong, wasn't I?" Tsuulo said. "About the Force. None of it was real. It was never with me." His gaze had become unfocused, as though he was looking through Han instead of at him.

Something pounded against the bulkhead door.

"I dunno. I . . ." Han was torn between trying to comfort his friend and making a run for it. The Kaldana would come through that door any second.

Suddenly, Qi'ra was at Tsuulo's side. She grabbed the sides of his head and pulled him to her so that their foreheads met. "The Force is real, Tsuulo. It's been with you the whole time. It's the only reason we made it this far."

"Really?"

"Really. Thank you."

He sighed. "Qi'ra. Tell Reezo . . . tell my brother I'm sorry . . . about the speeder. . . ." Tsuulo's head fell to his chest. His breathing stilled.

A giant hole was opening up where Han's chest used to be. A huge black hole that was going to swallow him and this ship and the entire galaxy.

Something tugged on his hand. "Han, we have to go. Tsuulo's dead."

No, it wasn't a hole at all; he'd been wrong about that. It was rage. White-hot blinding rage. Something exploded from his chest, a primal scream that echoed everywhere. Han rushed the bulkhead door and pounded it with his fists, his feet, his shoulder.

"Han! Please!"

He fell to his knees, vaguely aware that he'd hurt himself. His fingertips met blood, and he thought it was his, but no. Tsuulo's blood. His friend was dead.

Something got through to him, Qi'ra's pleading voice perhaps. He had another friend, someone who still needed his help.

Han jumped to his feet. "Let's go," he said gruffly.

Qi'ra loosed a breath of relief. "This way," she said, tearing down the corridor. They passed some storage lockers, a small repair bay, and finally turned right into a short, low hallway that dead-ended at a small door.

"Escape hatch," said Han.

They skidded to a halt. The door gave Han a slight start. Its shape and inset reminded him of the sewer openings beneath the streets of Corellia.

Qi'ra tried to palm it open, but it wouldn't budge.

Han stared at Tsuulo's datapad. There was a way past that door. There had to be.

A distant crash sounded. The Kaldana were coming through the bulkhead.

CHAPTER 21

Qi'ra watched helplessly while Han fiddled with the datapad and cable that Tsuulo had given him. If this didn't work, they were dead. There was nowhere left to go.

Han crouched and managed to get the datapad connected to the access terminal, but he was moving too slowly. No, not slowly. He had frozen.

Blood spattered the face of the datapad. Han was staring at it, unable to type.

"Let me take care of that," she said softly. She bunched up her sleeve in her hand, then she reached over and wiped the datapad clean. "There, it should be good now. But we've got to hurry."

He swallowed hard. "Right."

Han started typing quickly, but she had no idea if he knew what he was doing. *Come on, Qi'ra, think.* Maybe there *was* another way off this ship. The Kaldana had agreed they would transport Han and Qi'ra back to Corellia on a shuttle. That meant they had a shuttle.

She closed her eyes, recalling the map she'd seen on

the wall. She'd always been good at committing things to visual memory, and she could clearly remember another cargo bay on level one. Maybe the shuttle was there.

Then again, it was entirely likely the Kaldana had been lying about the shuttle.

Running footsteps approached.

"Han!"

"I think I can figure this out," he muttered, his fingers flying over the datapad.

"Maybe we should make a run for it. Try to find their shuttle."

"No, I've almost . . ."

Someone yelled, "This alien thing is dead."

"Good riddance," said another.

Qi'ra had never actually wished someone dead before. Until now. Now she wanted to kill every single Kaldana pirate she'd ever seen. With her bare hands.

"I think they're headed for the escape pod," someone said.

"*Han!*"

"I just have to believe I can do it. I just have to . . . There!" The door to the escape pod slid open.

"You did it!" she said.

"I did it!" His hands were shaking, his knuckles bruised and bloody from beating the bulkhead door. "I can't believe that worked."

"Celebrate later. Inside, now!" She shoved him through the door.

Han hadn't disconnected the cable yet. The datapad was still in his hand as he fell into the escape pod, and it disengaged, leaving the cable snaking on the ground.

Kaldana poured around the corner. The first one dropped to his knee and aimed his blaster.

Qi'ra dove for the escape pod. Her legs tangled in the cable. She tripped, lurching forward. Her temple banged against the side of the door, and she crumpled into a heap.

Blaster fire erupted where her head had just been.

She no longer knew up from down. Red tunneled her vision, and the side of her head throbbed. It hurt too much to even think. All she knew was that Han was inside the pod and she was outside and the Kaldana were right on top of them.

This was what it felt like to die. She reached feebly for the access panel. If she could jettison the pod, at least Han would get away. But she couldn't find it. He'd probably jettisoned already. Left her behind. It's what she would have done.

Qi'ra was alone. Totally, completely alone.

She closed her eyes, gathering strength. She'd get to her feet somehow. She'd go down fighting. She'd—

Hands grasped for her. Blaster fire sizzled the air. She felt herself being lifted, dragged over the lip of the doorway. Air hit her face as the hatch slammed shut.

"No time to buckle in," came a familiar voice. A voice she liked. "So stay flat on the floor. Try to hold on to one of the chairs. This might hurt."

Vaguely, through cloudy vision, she saw a fist hammer down on the eject button.

The ship expelled them with bone-numbing force. Her body slid across the floor and crashed into the wall. Then they were spinning, spinning, spinning. Her shoulder hit the ceiling, and her thigh smashed into a jump seat, and she knew, even with concussed thoughts, that one more bad blow would truly be her death.

And suddenly, arms were around her, cradling her, protecting her, and though she was still pummeled, the blows were softened. Survivable.

The escape pod leveled out as the maneuvering jets kicked in. Instead of being thrown around like rag dolls, they were floating through space, lighter than clouds in the wind.

"This pod doesn't have grav, so we'll have to strap ourselves in," Han said.

Han. He'd come back for her.

Strong arms used handholds and the edges of a jump

seat to guide them into place. He pushed her toward the seat, grabbed the straps, and gently, patiently belted her in.

He did the same for himself, settling in beside her. There was blood on his forehead. And his upper arm. She blinked, trying to clear her vision and assess the damage.

"Qi'ra? You okay?"

"You're bleeding."

"It's fine. You hit your head pretty bad back there, huh? Maybe you should—"

"I think I'm going to pass out now," she mumbled.

And that's what she did.

When she came to, she knew for certain she wasn't dead, because she had the absolute worst headache of her life.

"Qi'ra? Qi'ra! Holy moons, what a relief." Hands grabbed her chin, turned her head. "How many fingers am I holding up?"

"Han, get your hand out of my face."

He dropped his hand, but he was grinning so huge it practically split his dumb face. "I thought, I mean I was worried that . . ." His grin disappeared. "After Tsuulo, I couldn't lose . . ."

"You came back for me. You didn't leave me behind."

Han gave her a strange look. As though she'd just said something ridiculous like "Wookiees have wings."

"Of course I came back for you," he said. "Qi'ra, you're my friend. I would never leave you."

His words gutted her. No one had ever done that for her. Ever. Everyone, given the right circumstances, had chosen to betray her, to leave her behind. But not Han. He'd come back. At risk to his own life.

She hardly knew what she was doing as she reached for his hand. His fingers entwined with hers and held tight. "Thank you," she said.

"I'm just . . ." His expression grew agonized, and he whispered, "I wish Tsuulo . . . He was right there, Qi'ra. And suddenly, he wasn't."

"Me too." For a brief moment back on the Kaldana ship, Qi'ra had entertained the notion that when this was all over and she was safely back on Corellia, she'd have two people in all the world she could consider true friends. Now there was only Han.

"Did you mean what you said?" he asked.

"About what?"

"To Tsuulo. About the Force being real."

"No. I don't know. It just seemed like the right thing to say."

He sighed. "I figured. It was all just a bunch of mumbo jumbo."

"If it brought him comfort in the end, I guess that's something, right?"

"Sure. I guess."

Qi'ra would not cry. She would *not*. "I'm really going to miss him," she managed.

"Yeah, me too."

Before them was a small viewport. The pod's jets were guiding them wide of the moon, and Corellia was already in sight. It was beautiful from here, perfect blue with swirling white clouds. In the southern hemisphere, where the clouds weren't so dense, a city complex spread wide like a silver bug with multiple legs, hugging the continent.

"Is that Coronet City?" Qi'ra asked.

"I have no idea. Maybe."

"You think the Kaldana ship will come after us?"

"Maybe. Maybe not. Their ship wasn't exactly maneuverable. They might decide we're not worth the trouble."

Qi'ra leaned back into her jump seat and closed her eyes. The banging in her head was awful. And with maneuvering jets only, their ride to Corellia could take hours. Maybe a day.

She almost jumped when Han spoke again. "Can I ask you something?"

"Sure."

"Why did you turn down Jenra's offer?"

"It's hard to explain."

"I was sure you'd take it. I mean, you're so practical. That job would have given you food and nice things and—"

"You're a bad influence."

"Huh?"

"I turned her down because of you, okay? Happy now? I've been running around with you too much. I didn't like the way she looked at me . . . the way she looked at that Wookiee, talked about him like he was just a thing. . . . It gave me a bad feeling. So I trusted my gut. Just this once."

Han threw his head back and laughed.

"Shut up," she said, trying to glare and failing. "Hey, I happen to believe you can tell a lot about someone by the way they look at you. Lady Proxima, for example."

Han sobered and said, "Like you're a tasty piece of meat."

"Exactly."

"What about me?" he asked, his brown eyes suddenly intense, that cocky grin curving his lips. She didn't hate it anymore. She quite liked it, actually. Han had the face of a true friend. "How do *I* look at you?"

Qi'ra blinked. "Like you're trying your best to annoy me."

He shrugged. "Well, I can't deny that."

They were still holding hands, and neither seemed ready to let go. The fact that she could hold someone's hand without wanting to wrench away, without feeling as though she was giving too much of herself, gave her the courage to say, "Han, I don't want to be a White Worm anymore."

"Me neither," he said. "But it's what we've got. It's always been better than some—most? all?—of the alternatives."

"Or being in the Silo."

"Or that. I know what you mean, though," Han said. "The galaxy is a wide-open place. Bigger and more amazing than I ever imagined. It's going to be hard to go back down there, where everything is small and dirty and dark. Seems like there's a lot more to life than that. Or there ought to be, anyway."

She squeezed his hand. "I *liked* being up here. I liked being part of a high-stakes game. Making things happen. It was terrifying. But it was . . . fun."

"You like being a player."

"Yeah, maybe. Seems to me that being a player is the best way to survive. Having money. Influence. That's what keeps you flying."

Han shook his head. "What keeps you flying is having one person in all the galaxy to fly with. Someone you can trust to have your back. I mean, we wouldn't have survived any of this without each other."

"And Tsuulo."

"Yeah." A muscle in his neck moved. "I just wish we could have . . . gotten"—he swallowed hard—"his body. Brought it back to his brother or something."

They were silent a moment, considering. Then Qi'ra brightened with a thought. "Han, let's escape."

"Huh? Escape from the escape pod?"

"No, I mean from Lady Proxima and the White Worms. Somehow. We're smart. If we make it back to the planet, I say we figure something out. It might take some time, but—"

"I'm in." He was grinning again. "I'm totally in. In fact, let's leave Corellia altogether. I'm sure if we keep our eyes open for a good opportunity—"

"Han, no! You have to let me *plan* this."

"Yeah, yeah, sure."

She glared at him, but she felt herself lighting up inside. They were going to get away. Leave the White Worms behind forever. Somehow.

"Wait," Han said, pointing out the viewport. His shoulders slumped in despair.

A metallic monstrosity was sliding into view, ungainly with attachments, scarred by battle. Two huge turrets at the fore pivoted toward them.

"Oh, hells," Qi'ra said as all the joy she'd briefly allowed herself evaporated. "Those guys don't give up." Well, that would teach her to embrace any kind of hope. Just when she thought they would actually make it back alive, here came the Kaldana to blow them to smithereens.

Han's face was despondent. "This pod . . . it only has maneuvering jets. I guess I could make some small adjustments, but . . ." The hopelessness in his voice went straight to Qi'ra's heart.

"But we can't dodge torpedoes."

"Not without thrusters."

"So this is it, then."

"Qi'ra, I'm sorry." They were still holding hands. He turned his face to her and gazed deeply, as if memorizing her features.

"It's not your fault. It just is." Qi'ra reached up with her free hand and brushed her fingers along his cheek. Then she smiled.

"What's so funny?" he barked angrily.

"The burn on your face. It's finally peeling."

"Oh. Yeah." He reached up and scratched. "It's been itchy." Then he sighed dramatically. "At least I'll die with my good looks returning."

"I'm so relieved for you."

"Qi'ra, I'm glad I'm not alone right now."

"Yeah, me too."

Light poured into their escape pod, drenching Han's face in purest white. It seared Qi'ra's eyes, sending tears streaming down her face.

Against her better judgment, she turned toward the viewport, expecting to see a torpedo exploding against their hull. If she was going to die here, she would do it with her eyes wide open, just like Tsuulo.

But instead of ordnance, she saw . . . *nothing.*

The Kaldana ship was no longer there. It had been blown to bits.

She had a split second to register a glittering wash of debris floating through space, along with the glorious realization that they were alive. Then a shock wave hit, knocking her head against her jump seat.

The flesh of her cheeks pressed against her skull as the pod flew backward into a tailspin. Her teeth ground together, and her spine felt as if it were collapsing. She wanted to tell Han to hold on, that the pod would right itself, but too much pressure on her diaphragm made it impossible to breathe.

Their spin slowed. Stopped. All the stress on Qi'ra's bones lifted, her body becoming weightless once again. The jets reoriented, sending them back in the direction of Corellia, which the pod's programming had identified as the nearest habitable celestial body.

After a moment spent sucking in air, Han said, "What the hell just happened?"

Qi'ra shook her head. "I don't know. I just . . ." Her head was pounding, and every breath sent daggers through her neck and chest. But each pulse of pain felt like a gift. She was *alive*. "Maybe that junker was in even worse shape than we thought."

Han's expression seemed doubtful. "Maybe."

Another ship slid into view, sleek and shimmering with reflection, a red glow lighting its undercarriage.

"The *Red Nimbus*!" Qi'ra said.

"The Engineer destroyed the ship," Han said.

"Actually, I think she destroyed the entire Kaldana Syndicate." With the loss of their flagship, and over a billion credits, only a few dregs of the pirate organization would remain.

Han whistled. "No more shield tech. No more Kaldana. The Corellian skies are safe."

Qi'ra raised an eyebrow at him. "The Corellian skies will never be *safe*," she said.

"Fair point. Though . . ." Han frowned, thinking hard. "That was an awful lot of people who just died."

"Better them than us."

The red lighting of the *Nimbus* flickered once, then twice. As if signaling them. Or maybe saying good-bye. Then space seemed to fold on itself for the briefest moment, and in a blink, the *Nimbus* was gone, disappeared into hyperspace.

"It was a brilliant double cross," Qi'ra mused. "But I don't see a benefit to her. Why did she do it?"

Han shrugged. "I think she liked us. Especially you. So she decided to save us."

"Huh. Maybe."

"You know, that was a pretty nice funeral pyre," Han said. "For Tsuulo, I mean. Better than anything the White Worms would have done for him."

That was a kind thought. "Maybe he's back with the Force or whatever," Qi'ra said.

"Well, he's with the stars, at least."

Qi'ra put her head back, content for her hand to remain in Han's as Corellia loomed larger and larger before them.

CHAPTER 22

Han was late—again. This time Qi'ra was with him, and they had one last stop to make before returning to the White Worm den.

"This better be worth it," Qi'ra warned as she jogged beside him through the sewer tunnel. Their boots splashed through water and muck, and the faint blue light of morning filtered down from the street drains above. "We're already missing breakfast. If we're late to the meeting afterward . . ."

"We won't be," Han said. "We'll take the shortcut through Old Man Powlo's territory. It'll be fine."

"If you say so."

Han slowed his pace for her, hoping Qi'ra wouldn't notice. It's not that she wasn't right; they were definitely late, and missing the meeting would ruin all their plans. But their ride back to Corellia in the escape pod had been rough—rough enough that Qi'ra now sported a sling for her left shoulder, which had been wrenched out of socket when they hit the atmosphere. The pod had been as ancient and derelict as the ship it ejected from, without modern compensators and cooling protocols.

Now the pod was a burned-out husk, resting a few klicks east of the freighter boneyard. Bruised and battered, they'd stumbled to Qi'ra's safe house. The next day, they made the slow journey on foot back to the White Worm lair, where, true to her word, Lady Proxima had welcomed them home.

That had been two days before, and they were still battered and exhausted.

Now that things were back to normal, Lady Proxima announced that she'd decided who would receive the promotion of Head. She would reveal the lucky Worm at a meeting after breakfast. All candidates were instructed to be present and on time.

For their plan of escape to have any chance of succeeding, either Han or Qi'ra had to win the position.

"Here we are," Han said. He cranked the wheel of the blast door. It squealed like a dying rat, making Qi'ra wince. Together, they stepped inside and ascended the stairs. Han couldn't help thinking of the first time he'd climbed these stairs, when a deal had gone bad and blaster fire had nearly taken his head off. Tool had saved him that day.

The droid was inside waiting for them, standing tall against the wall, two of his attachments crossed like human arms. One of them was new. A golden alloy in bright contrast to the rest of his hulking steel frame. Most notable though were the holo-flames, licking and flickering all about his carapace, making the droid appear as though he burned with soft blue fire.

"Tool!" Han said. "You look great!"

"I do, don't I," he intoned.

"Glad to see you, Tool," Qi'ra said.

"And you, Qi'ra. Please sit if it will make you comfortable." Tool made a sweeping gesture with his lathe that Han assumed was meant to be welcoming. The room had been cleaned of blood and spilled guts, the chairs and table righted, but neither moved to sit.

"We're good," Qi'ra said. "You said in your message you had something for us? A reward?"

Han gave her the side-eye. It wasn't like her to rush a deal. She must really be worried about being late. But she'd agreed to come because they needed that reward, whatever it was. The first step to escaping Lady Proxima and the White Worms was acquiring resources.

"Yes, you see the Kaldana Syndicate almost got away with that shield tech, which they would have used to utterly destroy our organization."

"I'm glad that didn't happen, Tool," Han said in all sincerity. "Your cause is a lot safer now."

"Only because after we lost the bid, we back-channeled the Engineer and cut a second, secret deal."

Qi'ra leaned forward. "Oh? What second deal? I didn't hear anything about—"

"Do you know the meaning of 'secret,'" Tool said.

"Tool, what was this secret deal?" Han demanded.

"We offered her three hundred thousand credits to destroy the Kaldana ship as soon as the exchange was complete."

Han's mouth dropped open as Qi'ra sucked in breath.

Han recovered first. "So she didn't come back to save us," he said.

"She blew that ship to bits for money," Qi'ra said. "Everything's always about money, isn't it?"

"She declined our offer at first," Tool told them. "She had no interest in who ended up with the technology, so long as she was paid and could escape free. She believed that staying behind a little while longer put her ship at risk."

Han could hardly fathom it. All those people dead—a whole syndicate—for only three hundred thousand credits. Better them than him and Qi'ra of course. Still, it felt wrong.

"What changed her mind?" Qi'ra asked.

"You did. She contacted us again during the exchange

and said three young scoundrels made her see things differently. So we transferred the money, and she blew up their ship and everyone in it. In the days since, we've pursued stragglers throughout the sector, taking them out one by one. In short, we have wiped them out."

"All of them?" Han practically squeaked.

"They were a scourge on the galaxy," Tool said.

Han and Qi'ra exchanged startled glances. The Kaldana captain had said the exact same thing about Rodians.

"That was a clever double cross," Qi'ra said. "Coldly practical."

Han gave her a confused look. It sounded like she admired them for it.

"Hey, it's better to be the betrayer than be the betrayed," she said.

"But . . . so many people," Han said.

"I care little for the death counts of organics," said Tool. "It's nothing like what droids have experienced."

Suddenly, Han was glad no one had gotten the shield technology. Not the Kaldana, not the White Worms, and especially not the Droid Gotra. Tool had almost convinced him their cause was worthy. Han had gone so far as to defend the Gotra to the Engineer.

Well, that would be the last time he got swindled into believing in a cause. *Cause* was just a fancy word for *war*, and war always got people killed, often innocent people. Like Tsuulo.

"My organization thanks you for being such loyal allies in the fight for droid equality," Tool continued. "We've decided to bestow a token of appreciation. It's a street speeder—"

Han gasped.

"—which we shall present to your Rodian friend."

Han's heart sunk.

"He saved me from nonfunction, and his technical skills allowed the datacube to stay out of enemy hands. Where is he? I expected him to join us."

"He's dead," Qi'ra said flatly. "The Kaldana killed him."

"Oh, that's too bad."

"Hey, we helped with all that stuff!" Han said. "We kept the datacube out of—"

"Yes, but mostly Tsuulo," Tool insisted. "I'm disappointed to hear of his demise. Does he have an heir?"

Qi'ra stepped forward. "*We* are his—"

Han put a hand on her arm. His voice was glum as he said, "His brother. He has a brother named Reezo who is in dire need of a speeder right now."

"Han!" Qi'ra protested. "We need resources."

"We'll figure something out. This is the right thing to do."

She glared at him. "I hate you."

"No, you don't."

Qi'ra sighed. "No. I don't. Tool, we'll make sure that speeder gets to Tsuulo's brother."

Tool inclined his head in a very human gesture. "The Droid Gotra thanks you."

Qi'ra led the way as they raced back to the White Worm lair. She hated being late. *Hated* it. The mess hall was empty when they arrived. "Blast," Qi'ra panted out.

"Just keep running." Han sprinted through the mess and its scattered tables to the tunnel leading to the Sinkhole. They burst through and skidded to a halt at the edge of Lady Proxima's scummy pond.

White Worms surrounded the pond, lining every bit of free wall space. Some sat in the upper adjoining tunnels, legs dangling over the edge. Morning light filtered thick and blue through the high clerestory windows. There were even more humans in the gang now, kids Han didn't recognize. Lady Proxima must have done some recruiting while they were gone.

Actually, she had probably recruited the humans to hunt them on the surface back when she still wanted all three of them dead.

Lady Proxima herself huddled in the center, half-submerged. Her jewelry glistened with dripping water, and her dominant arms were twitching with anticipation.

When she saw them, she emerged from the water, exposing her long wormy body and her tiny swimmerets, causing the water to lap at the concrete edges. As always, Qi'ra had to resist the urge to recoil. She was just so huge, taller even than Moloch.

"Qi'ra. Han," she said, in a voice meant to convey maternal affection, though it made Qi'ra feel like a juicy bug about to be squashed. "Just in time, my darlings."

"You commanded our presence, and we obeyed," Han said with a grin.

Rebolt stood off to the side, glaring at them. No doubt he'd been hoping they'd be late. Qi'ra wasn't sorry to disappoint.

His hounds were with him, massive grinning beasts with thick slimy hides the color of spoiled cream. They sat calmly, their giant heads reaching above Rebolt's waist. One licked at its paw. The other yawned, pointed tongue flicking in and out. Qi'ra knew they could jump to action at a single command from Rebolt.

"Now that all my darling children are here," Proxima said, "it's time to choose a new Head Child of the White

Worms. Rebolt, Qi'ra, and Han, please step forward."

They obeyed, stepping to the very edge of the pond.

Qi'ra stared straight ahead, her chin up, lips set stubbornly. She didn't want anyone to know how much she wanted this. How disappointed she'd be if she didn't get it. She was going to play it cool no matter what.

"I've narrowed my choice down to you three. Rebolt, you are loyal. Dangerous with those hounds. An enforcer."

Rebolt inclined his head in acknowledgment.

"Qi'ra, you are smart, observant, and strategic. A tactician."

All true, but Qi'ra did not respond in the slightest.

"And, Han, you are instinctive and lucky, liked by everyone around town. An ambassador."

Han shrugged. "It comes naturally."

Rebolt glared at him. Qi'ra failed to hide a smile.

But Lady Proxima's beakish mouth turned down into a frown. "And occasionally disrespectful," she added.

"Which is why," Han said loudly, his voice carrying, "you shouldn't pick me."

Rebolt gaped. Qi'ra mouthed, *What are you doing?*

Han straightened and addressed Lady Proxima as respectfully as Qi'ra had ever heard him speak to anyone: "Honored Lady, you should choose Qi'ra."

Qi'ra's eyebrows practically reached her hairline. A

hubbub arose as the White Worms crowding the Sinkhole began mumbling among themselves.

"It's the lady's decision, not yours," Rebolt said.

"Of course it is," Han said. "And since the job comes down to you or Qi'ra now, and you are supposedly the loyal one, then our beloved lady must know the truth."

"What truth?" said Proxima, looming closer.

"Yeah, what truth?" Rebolt demanded. One of his hounds sensed his tension and shifted on its hindquarters, growling low.

"When we were on assignment, Qi'ra received a job offer. Something that would allow her to see the whole galaxy. Maybe even make her rich. But she turned it down. Out of loyalty to you, Honored Lady."

Everyone gasped.

Qi'ra wasn't about to tell them that the facts were right but the motivation was wrong.

"Furthermore," Han continued, "she's the smartest person I've ever met. I wouldn't have survived that assignment if not for her. I would follow her lead anywhere, and so should everyone here."

As speeches went, it wasn't too bad. Especially for Han. He was more cut out for leadership than he realized. Even Qi'ra could see that.

Lady Proxima loomed over Qi'ra, then slowly, inexorably lowered herself until they were nose to nose. Her huge face dwarfed Qi'ra's, and her nostril slits twitched, as though she was sniffing the girl.

Qi'ra didn't move. Didn't even blink. She would be poised. She would not panic.

"Is it true, Qi'ra, my darling?" Proxima said. "Did you reject the whole galaxy for me?"

One heartbeat. Two.

"Yes, my lady. My home is here. With you."

Proxima drew herself to full height again, water sloshing everywhere. She clapped her dominant hands together, and her swimmerets waved with excitement. To everyone crowding the Sinkhole, she said, "Please welcome your new Head, Qi'ra of the White Worms!"

A cheer went up, and no one cheered more loudly than Han. Qi'ra felt vaguely stunned while kids surrounded her, slapping her back, shouting congratulations. Even Moloch inclined his head at her in acknowledgment.

Only Rebolt stood off to the side, seething, his hounds dancing with barely contained anxiety.

Lady Proxima waved her arms, and the crowd hushed.

She said, "In celebration, the mess will serve a second round of breakfast."

Another cheer. But Qi'ra couldn't quite bring herself to celebrate. She was too confused. *Why* had he done it?

Yum, thought Han as he headed to second breakfast. *More rat sludge.*

But this marked the beginning of Lady Proxima's keeping her end of the bargain and feeding them two meals per day, so Han wasn't about to complain. As they all herded themselves through the tunnel back into the mess, Qi'ra grabbed Rebolt's sleeve.

"Rebolt," she said, and he spun to face her.

Everyone froze and stared, waiting to see what would happen. Han moved closer, ready to tackle Rebolt if he tried anything.

Rebolt hesitated before replying, "What?"

"I have an errand for you."

Horror filled Rebolt's face as the true import hit him. Qi'ra was in charge now. She could order him to do anything. A muscle in his jaw twitched. Then he managed, "Yes, Head. Whatever you need."

But he turned to glare coldly at Han.

Han smiled. He couldn't wait to hear what she'd cooked up.

"Take a few of your dog biscuits and deliver them to a friend of mine," she said. "His name is Powlo. Tell him it's in gratitude for helping Han, Qi'ra, and Tsuulo, for letting us visit."

Rebolt's eyes narrowed. "You mean Old Man Powlo? That creepy hermit?"

"Powlo is a great ally of the White Worms, and we shall continue to cultivate our relationship with him," Qi'ra said. Quickly, she gave him directions.

Rebolt turned to go.

"And, Rebolt!" Qi'ra called after him. He paused but did not turn around. "Don't scare him. Leave your hounds behind."

He stormed off, and Han felt his grin grow wider and wider. "He really hates us now," he observed.

"Oh, yes," Qi'ra said. "But he already did. I realized I had to put him in his place quick. Establish my authority. Be careful with him, Han. He'll blame you for all this."

That was Qi'ra, always thinking.

As they stepped into the mess, Han said, "Tsuulo would have loved to see that happen."

Qi'ra gifted him with a sad smile. "Yes, I think he would have."

They sat at one of the lily pad tables. A few others tried to join them, but Qi'ra waved them off. When no one was in earshot, she leaned forward and said, "Han, I have to know. Why did you do it? Was it just one of those impulse decisions?"

"Sort of. Maybe." The truth was, Qi'ra deserved the position. And it was more important to her than it was to him.

"But I thought you really wanted this."

"I did." He leaned close so their faces were a hand's breadth apart, and he whispered, "There are some things I want even more. Like escaping Corellia. With my only friend."

Her cheeks colored, and she sat back in her seat. A tiny smile curved her lips. "No one's ever sacrificed something for me before."

"Well, don't get used to it," he said gruffly, suddenly uncomfortable. "And I wouldn't have done it if you didn't deserve it."

She was still smiling. He loved that smile. "I think I finally believe you," she said. "You'll never betray me, will you, Han?"

"Course not."

A little boy no older than seven years old approached, wearing smudged goggles and carrying a bowl. Qi'ra started to wave him away, but the boy said, "I'm Hallro. I'm new. Moloch says you get a bowl of creamed herring now that you're Head."

"Oh. Uh, thanks, Hallro." Qi'ra sniffed it, shrugged, then took a bite. The boy in the goggles backed away.

"How is it?" Han asked.

"Creamy," she said. "And fishy."

"I guess it beats rat sludge."

"Barely. Here, have some." She shoved the bowl at him, and he didn't hesitate to take a huge bite.

It wasn't awful. "So," he said, wiping his mouth, "you're sharing your special ration with me. Just the two of us. Alone. Eating a meal together. Is this . . . a date?"

"No! Of course not."

You couldn't blame a guy for trying. If he was being honest with himself, he was a little relieved. What he needed right now was a friend. Even though Qi'ra just might be the prettiest, most interesting girl he had ever met.

Something in her face changed, and Han got the feeling she was holding back a smile. "But maybe . . . someday . . ." She let the idea dangle in the air.

Someday sounded good. "Yeah. Maybe." He gave her his most charming grin.

They ate in companionable silence, in the way of trusted friends who didn't need to fill a space with conversation. Han had meant what he said to Qi'ra in the escape pod. *What keeps you flying is having one person in all the galaxy to fly with. Someone you can trust to have your back.*

Qi'ra might be his one person. She would always have his back, and he would have hers. And together, someday soon, they would fly away.